# Mythistory
# and Other
# Essays

# Mythistory and Other Essays

# William H. McNeill

The University of Chicago Press
Chicago and London

William H. McNeill is the Robert A. Milliken Distinguished Service Professor of History at the University of Chicago. In 1964 McNeill received the National Book Award for *The Rise of the West: A History of the Human Community* (University of Chicago Press, 1963). His many other published works include *Venice, the Hinge of Europe*; *The Metamorphosis of Greece since World War II*; *The Pursuit of Power: Technology, Armed Force, and Society since A.D. 1000*; and *History of Western Civilization: A Handbook*, all published by the University of Chicago Press, and *Plagues and Peoples*; *The Human Condition: An Ecological and Historical View*; *The Great Frontier: Freedom and Hierarchy in Modern Times*; and others.

*Library of Congress Cataloging-in-Publication Data*

McNeill, William Hardy, 1917–
   Mythistory and other essays.

   Includes index.
   1. History—Philosophy—Addresses, essays, lectures.
   2. Historians—Addresses, essays, lectures.   I. Title.
   D16.8.M39   1986       901       85-8584
   ISBN 0-226-56135-6


The University of Chicago Press, Chicago 60637
The University of Chicago Press, Ltd., London
© 1986 by The University of Chicago
All rights reserved. Published 1986
Printed in the United States of America

95 94 93 92 91 90 89 88 87 86   54321

# Contents

# Preface

✳

As a young man, I thought methodology a waste of time: many words about questions which were either unanswerable, or could best be approached by performing the intellectual task in question instead of by talking about how to do it. But with the passage of time my attitude changed, slowly and imperceptibly at first, then more rapidly, so that by now I find it far easier to discourse about how to write history than to mount the sustained and concerted effort needed to produce a decent book or article. This collection of essays is, therefore, a minor monument to the process whereby this habit of mind has grown on me across the decades since I wrote an appraisal of Toynbee's *A Study of History* for the symposium at Loyola University that Edward Gargan organized in 1955.

It is also the product of injured vanity, for when Cornell University Press rejected the account of my encounters with Becker, Toynbee, and Braudel that I had prepared for the Becker lectures at Cornell in 1983, I sought some way of making those three essays more attractive to a publisher. Soon thereafter, I learned that I would be privileged to pontificate as president of the American Historical Association in 1985; and it occurred to me that by publishing my presidential address along with some other essays of a historiographical character that I had prepared for various occasions and published in diverse places, a publishable book might result. It would also give my presidential address a launching pad supplementary to that afforded by the usual publication in *The American Historical Review*.

The result is this little volume. The laziness and vanity that combined to generate it may not be much of a recommendation. Still, professional historians have been almost totally secretive about how their minds were formed. My effort to explain how time, place, and occasion determined what I was able to learn from my elders when I was young may therefore be indiscreet enough to interest some readers. Others may be at the fertile stage of intellectual growth when basic ideas and fundamental commitments take shape. For them, some of these words may really matter—provoking new thoughts, new perspectives, new doubts, and new certainties.

Most potential readers will have their minds already made up on all essential matters. They will therefore be irritated, puzzled, or amused by my idiosyncracies and eccentricities. Indeed, a friendly young critic remarked to me that I was in danger of developing a private language that would guarantee misunderstanding within the historical profession. This is indeed a risk; yet it is also the case that intellectual breakthroughs come when someone pushes hard against older limits and starts talking nonsense.

This is what I hope the essays in this book actually do. Whether that hope is well grounded will depend on how others react, or fail to react, to what I have to say. Really important texts are those susceptible of being richly and diversely misunderstood. An author can always aspire to that dignity. These essays, at least, point in that direction by inviting misunderstanding more than most.

William H. McNeill
April 1985

# Part One

## *Truth, Myth, and History*

# One

# Mythistory,
# or Truth, Myth, History,
# and Historians

Myth and history are close kin inasmuch as both explain how things got to be the way they are by telling some sort of story. But our common parlance reckons myth to be false while history is, or aspires to be, true. Accordingly, a historian who rejects someone else's conclusions calls them mythical, while claiming that his own views are true. But what seems true to one historian will seem false to another, so one historian's truth becomes another's myth, even at the moment of utterance.

A century and more ago, when history was first established as an academic discipline, our predecessors recognized this dilemma, and believed they had a remedy. Scientific source criticism would get the facts

Prepared as the presidential address for the American Historical Association's annual meeting, December 1985.

straight, whereupon a conscientious and careful historian needed only to arrange the facts into a readable narrative to produce genuinely scientific history. And science, of course, like the stars above, was true and eternal, as Newton and Laplace had demonstrated to the satisfaction of all reasonable persons everywhere.

Yet in practice, revisionism continued to prevail within the newly constituted historical profession, as it had since the time of Herodotus. For a generation or two, this continued volatility could be attributed to scholarly success in discovering new facts by diligent work in the archives; but early in this century thoughtful historians began to realize that the arrangement of facts to make a history involved subjective judgments and intellectual choices that had little or nothing to do with source criticism, scientific or otherwise.

In reacting against an almost mechanical vision of scientific method it is easy to underestimate actual achievements. For the ideal of scientific history did allow our predecessors to put some forms of bias behind them. In particular, academic historians of the nineteenth century came close to transcending older religious controversies. Protestant and Catholic histories of post-Reformation Europe ceased to be separate and distinct traditions of learning—a transformation nicely illustrated in the Anglo-American world by the career of Lord Acton, a Roman Catholic who became Regius Professor of History at Cambridge and editor of the first *Cambridge Modern History*. This was a great accomplishment. So was the accumulation of an enormous fund of exact and reliable data through painstaking source criticism that allowed the writing of history in the western world to assume a new depth, scope, range, and precision as compared to anything possible in earlier times. No heir of that scholarly tradition should scoff at the faith of our predecessors which inspired so much toiling in archives.

Yet the limits of scientific history were far more constricting than its devotees believed. Facts that could be established beyond all reasonable doubt remained trivial in the sense that they did not, in and of themselves, give meaning or intelligibility to the record of the past. A catalogue of undoubted and indubitable information, even if arranged chronologically, remains a catalogue. To become a history, facts have to be put together into a pattern that is understandable and credible; and when that has been achieved, the resulting portrait of the past may become useful as well—a font of practical wisdom upon which people may draw when making decisions and taking action.

Pattern recognition of the sort historians engage in is the chef d'oeuvre of human intelligence. It is achieved by paying selective attention to the total input of stimuli that perpetually swarm in upon our consciousness. Only by leaving things out, i.e., relegating them to the status of background noise deserving only to be disregarded, can what matters most in a given situation become recognizable. Suitable action follows. Here is the great secret of human power over nature and over ourselves as well. Pattern recognition is what natural scientists are up to; it is what historians have always done, whether they knew it or not.

Only some facts matter for any given pattern. Otherwise useless clutter will obscure what we are after: perceptible relationships among important facts. That and that alone constitutes an intelligible pattern, giving meaning to the world, whether it be the world of physics and chemistry or the world of interacting human groups through time, which historians take as their special domain. Natural scientists are ruthless in selecting aspects of available sensory inputs to pay attention to, disregarding all else. They call their patterns theories, and inherit most of them from predecessors. But, as we now know, even Newton's truths needed adjustment. Natural science is neither eternal nor universal; it is instead historical and evolutionary, because scientists accept a new theory only when the new embraces a wider range of phenomena or achieves a more elegant explanation of (selectively observed) facts than its predecessor was able to do.

No comparably firm consensus prevails among historians. Yet we need not despair. The great and obvious difference between natural scientists and historians is the greater complexity of the behavior historians seek to understand. The principal source of historical complexity lies in the fact that human beings react both to the natural world and to one another chiefly through the mediation of symbols. This means, among other things, that any theory about human life, if widely believed, will alter actual behavior, usually by inducing people to act as if the theory were true. Ideas and ideals thus become self-validating within remarkably elastic limits. An extraordinary behavioral motility results. Resort to symbols, in effect, loosened up the connection between external reality and human responses, freeing us from instinct by setting us adrift on a sea of uncertainty. Human beings thereby acquired a new capacity to err, but also to change, adapt, and learn new ways of doing things. Innumerable errors, corrected by experience, eventually made us lords of creation as no other species on earth has ever been before.

The price of this achievement is the elastic, inexact character of truth, and especially of truths about human conduct. What a particular group of persons understands, believes, and acts upon, even if quite absurd to outsiders, may nonetheless cement social relations and allow the members of the group to act together and accomplish feats otherwise impossible. Moreover, membership in such a group and participation in its sufferings and triumphs give meaning and value to individual human lives. Any other sort of life is not worth living, for we are social creatures. As such we need to share truths with one another, and not just truths about atoms, stars, and molecules, but about human relations and the people around us.

Shared truths that provide a sanction for common effort have obvious survival value. Without such social cement no group can long preserve itself. Yet to outsiders, truths of this kind are likely to seem myths, save in those (relatively rare) cases when the outsider is susceptible to conversion and finds a welcome within the particular group in question.

The historic record available to us consists of an unending appearance and dissolution of human groups, each united by its own beliefs, ideals, and traditions. Sects, religions, tribes, and states, from ancient Sumer and Pharaonic Egypt to modern times, have based their cohesion upon shared truths—truths that differed from time to time and place to place with a rich and reckless variety. Today the human community remains divided among an enormous number of different groups, each espousing its own version of truth about itself, and about those excluded from its fellowship. Everything suggests that this sort of social and ideological fragmentation will continue indefinitely.

Where, in such a maelstrom of conflicting opinions, can we hope to locate historical truth? Where indeed?

Before modern communications thrust familiarity with the variety of human idea-systems upon our consciousness, this question was not particularly acute. Individuals nearly always grew up in relatively isolated communities to a more or less homogeneous world view. Important questions had been settled long ago by prophets and sages, so there was little reason to challenge or modify traditional wisdom. Indeed there were strong positive restraints upon any would-be innovator who threatened to upset the inherited consensus.

To be sure, climates of opinion fluctuated, but changes came surreptitiously, usually disguised as commentary upon old texts, and purporting merely to explicate the original meanings. Flexibility was considerable, as the modern practice of the U.S. Supreme Court should convince us; but in this traditional ordering of intellect, all the same, outsiders who did not share the prevailing orthodoxy were shunned and disregarded when they could not be converted. Our predecessors' faith in a scientific method that would make written history absolutely and universally true was no more than a recent example of such a belief system. Those who embraced it felt no need to pay attention to ignoramuses who had not accepted the truths of "modern science." Like other true believers, they were therefore spared the task of taking others' viewpoints seriously, or wondering about the limits of their own vision of historical truth.

But we are denied the luxury of such parochialism. We must reckon with multiplex, competing faiths—secular as well as transcendental, revolutionary as well as traditional—that resound amongst us. In addition, partially autonomous professional idea-systems have proliferated in the past century or so. Those most important to historians are the so-called social sciences—anthropology, sociology, political science, psychology, and economics—together with the newer disciplines of ecology and semeiology. But law, theology, and philosophy also pervade the field of knowledge with which historians may be expected to deal. On top of all this, innumerable individual authors, each with his own assortment of ideas and assumptions, compete for attention. Choice is everywhere; dissent turns into cacaphonous confusion; my truth dissolves into your myth even before I can put words on paper.

The liberal faith, of course, holds that in a free marketplace of ideas, Truth will eventually prevail. I am not ready to abandon that faith, however dismaying our present confusion may be. The liberal experiment, after all, is only about two hundred and fifty years old, and on the appropriate world-historical time scale that is too soon to be sure. Still, confusion is undoubted. Whether the resulting uncertainty will be bearable for large numbers of people in difficult times ahead is a question worth asking. Iranian Moslems, Russian Communists, and American sectarians (religious and otherwise) all exhibit symptoms of acute distress in face of moral uncertainties, generated by exposure to competing truths. Clearly, the will to believe is as strong today as at any time in the past; and true believers nearly always wish to create a community of the faithful, so as to be able to live more comfortably, insulated from troublesome dissent.

The prevailing response to an increasingly cosmopolitan confusion has been intensified personal attachment, first to national, and then to subnational groups, each with its own distinct ideals and practices. As one would expect, the historical profession faithfully reflected and helped to forward these shifts of sentiment. Thus, the founding fathers of the American Historical Association and their immediate successors were intent on facilitating the consolidation of a new American nation by writing national history in a WASPish mold, while also claiming affiliation with a tradition of Western civilization that ran back through modern and medieval Europe to the ancient Greeks and Hebrews. This version of our past was very widely repudiated in the 1960s, but iconoclastic revisionists felt no need to replace what they attacked with any architectonic vision of their own. Instead, scholarly energy concentrated on discovering the history of various segments of the population that had been left out or ill-treated by older historians: most notably women, Blacks, and other ethnic minorities within the United States, and the ex-colonial peoples of the world beyond the national borders.

Such activity conformed to our traditional professional role of helping to define collective identities in ambiguous situations. Consciousness of a common past, after all, is a powerful supplement to other ways of defining who "we" are. An oral tradition, sometimes almost undifferentiated from the practical wisdom embodied in language itself, is all people need in a stable social universe where in-group boundaries are self-evident. But with civilization, ambiguities multiplied, and formal written history became useful in defining "us" versus "them." At first, the central ambiguity ran between rulers and ruled. Alien conquerors who lived on taxes collected from their subjects were at best a necessary evil when looked at from the bottom of civilized society. Yet in some situations, especially when confronting natural disaster or external attack, a case could be made for commonality, even between taxpayers and tax consumers. At any rate, histories began as king lists, royal genealogies and boasts of divine favor: obvious ways of consolidating rulers' morale and asserting their legitimacy vis-à-vis their subjects.

Jewish history emphasized God's power over human affairs, narrowing the gap between rulers and ruled by subjecting everybody to divine Providence. The Greeks declared all free men equal, subject to no one, but bound by a common obedience to law. The survival value of both these visions of the human condition is fairly obvious. A people united by their fear and love of God have an ever present help in time of trouble, as Jewish history surely proves. Morale can survive disaster, time and again; internal disputes and differences diminish beneath the weight of a shared subjection to God. The Greek ideal of freedom under law is no less practical in the sense that willing cooperation is likely to elicit maximal collective effort, whether in war or peace.

Interplay between these two ideals runs throughout the history of western civilization, but this is not the place to enter into a detailed historiographical analysis. Let me merely remark that our professional heritage from the liberal and nationalist historiography of the nineteenth century drew mainly on the Greek, Herodotean model, emphasizing the supreme value of political freedom within a territorially defined state.

World War I constituted a catastrophe for that liberal and nationalist vision of human affairs, since freedom that permitted such costly and lethal combat no longer seemed a plausible culmination of all historic experience. Boom, bust, and World War II did nothing to clarify the issue, and the multiplication of sub-national historiographies since the 1950s merely increased our professional confusion.

What about truth amidst all this weakening of old certainties, florescence of new themes, and widening of sensibilities? What really and truly matters? What should we pay attention to? What must we neglect?

All human groups like to be flattered. Historians are therefore under perpetual temptation to conform to expectation by portraying the people they write about as they wish to be. A mingling of truth and falsehood, blending history with ideology, results. Historians are likely to select facts to show that we—whoever "we" may be—conform to our cherished principles: that we are free with Herodotus, or saved with Augustine, or oppressed with Marx, as the case may be. Grubby details indicating that the group fell short of its ideals can be skated over or omitted entirely. The result is mythical: the past as we want it to be, safely simplified into a contest between good guys and bad guys, "us" and "them." Most national history and most group history is of this kind, though the intensity of chiaroscuro varies greatly, and sometimes an historian turns traitor to the group he studies by setting out to unmask its pretentions. Groups struggling towards self-consciousness and groups whose accustomed status seems threatened are likely to demand (and get) vivid, simplified portraits of their admirable virtues and undeserved sufferings. Groups accustomed to power and surer of their internal cohesion can afford to accept more subtly modulated portraits of their successes and failures in bringing practice into conformity with principles.

Historians respond to this sort of market by expressing varying degrees of commitment to, and detachment from, the causes they chronicle, and by infusing varying degrees of emotional intensity into their pages through particular choices of words. Truth, persuasiveness, intelligibility rest far more on this level of the historian's art than on source criticism. But, as I said at the beginning, one person's truth is another's myth, and the fact that a group of people accept a given version of the past does not make that version any truer for outsiders.

Yet we cannot afford to reject collective self-flattery as silly, contemptible error. Myths are, after all, often self-validating. A nation or any other human group that knows how to behave in crisis situations because it has inherited a heroic historiographical tradition that tells how ancestors resisted their enemies successfully is more likely to act together effectively than a group lacking such a tradition. Great Britain's conduct in 1940 shows how world politics can be redirected by such a heritage. Flattering historiography does more than assist a given group to survive by affecting the balance of power among warring peoples, for an appropriately idealized version of the past may also allow a group of human beings to come closer to living up to its noblest ideals. What is can move towards what ought to be, given collective commitment to a flattering self-image. The American civil rights movement of the fifties and sixties illustrates this phenomenon amongst us.

These collective manifestations are of very great importance. Belief in the virtue and righteousness of one's cause is a necessary sort of self-delusion for human beings, singly and collectively. A corrosive version of history that emphasizes all the recurrent discrepancies between ideal and reality in a given group's behavior makes it harder for members of the group in question to act cohesively and in good conscience. That sort of history is very costly indeed. No group can afford it for long.

On the other hand, myths may mislead disastrously. A portrait of the past that denigrates others and praises the ideals and practice of a given group naively and without restraint, can distort a people's image of outsiders so that foreign relations begin to consist of nothing but nasty surprises. Confidence in one's own high principles and good intentions may simply provoke others to resist duly accredited missionaries of the true faith, whatever that faith may be. Both the United States and the Soviet Union have encountered their share of this sort of surprise and disappointment ever since 1917, when Wilson and Lenin proclaimed their respective recipes for curing the world's ills. In more extreme cases, mythical, self-flattering versions of the past may push a people towards suicidal behavior, as Hitler's last days may remind us.

More generally, it is obvious that mythical, self-flattering versions of rival groups' pasts simply serve to intensify their capacity for conflict. With the recent quantum jump in the destructive power of weaponry, hardening of group cohesion at the sovereign state level clearly threatens the survival of humanity; while within national borders, the civic order experiences new strains when subnational groups acquire a historiography replete with oppressors living next door and, perchance, still enjoying the fruits of past injustices.

The great historians have always responded to these difficulties by expanding their sympathies beyond narrow in-group boundaries. Herodotus set out to award a due meed of glory both to Hellenes and to the barbarians; Ranke inquired after what really happened to Protestant and Catholic, Latin and German nations alike. And other pioneers of our profession have likewise expanded the range of their sympathies and sensibilities beyond previously recognized limits without ever entirely escaping, or even wishing to escape, from the sort of partisanship involved in accepting the general assumptions and beliefs of a particular time and place.

Where to fix one's loyalties is the supreme question

of human life, and is especially acute in a cosmopolitan age like ours when choices abound. Belonging to a tightly knit group makes life worth living by giving individuals something beyond the self to serve and to rely on for personal guidance, companionship and aid. But the stronger such bonds, the sharper the break with the rest of humanity. Group solidarity is always maintained, at least partly, by exporting psychic frictions across the frontiers, projecting animosities onto an outside foe in order to enhance collective cohesion within the group itself. Indeed, something to fear, hate, and attack is probably necessary for the full expression of human emotions; and ever since animal predators ceased to threaten, human beings have feared, hated, and fought one another.

Historians, by helping to define "us" and "them," play a considerable part in focusing love and hate, the two principal cements of collective behavior known to humanity. But myth making for rival groups has become a dangerous game in the atomic age, and we may well ask whether there is any alternative open to us.

In principle the answer is obvious. Humanity entire possesses a commonality which historians may hope to understand just as firmly as they can comprehend what unites any lesser group. Instead of enhancing conflicts, as parochial historiography inevitably does, an intelligible world history might be expected to diminish the lethality of group encounters by cultivating a sense of individual identification with the triumphs and tribulations of humanity as a whole. This, indeed, strikes me as the moral duty of the historical profession in our time. We need to develop an ecumenical history, with plenty of room for human diversity in all its complexity.

Yet a wise historian will not denigrate intense attachment to small groups. That is essential to personal happiness. In all civilized societies, a tangle of overlapping social groupings lays claim to human loyalties. Any one person may therefore be expected to have multiple commitments and plural public identities, up to and including membership in the human race and the wider DNA community of life on planet Earth. What we need to do as historians and as human beings is to recognize this complexity, and balance our loyalties so that no one group will be able to command total commitment. Only so can we hope to make the world safer for all the different human groups that now exist and may come into existence.

The historical profession has, however, shied away from an ecumenical view of the human adventure. Professional career patterns reward specialization; and in all the well-trodden fields, where pervasive consensus on important matters has already been achieved, research and innovation necessarily concentrate upon minutiae. Residual faith that truth somehow resides in original documents confirms this direction of our energies. An easy and commonly unexamined corollary is the assumption that world history is too vague and too general to be true; i.e., accurate to the sources. Truth, according to this view, is only attainable on a tiny scale when the diligent historian succeeds in exhausting the relevant documents before they exhaust the historian.

But as my previous remarks have made clear, this does not strike me as a valid view of historical method. On the contrary, I call it naive and erroneous.

All truths are general. All truths abstract from the available assortment of data simply by using words, which in their very nature generalize so as to bring order to the incessantly fluctuating flow of messages in and messages out that constitutes human consciousness. Total reproduction of experience is impossible and undesirable. It would merely perpetuate the confusion we seek to escape. Historiography that aspires to get closer and closer to the documents—all the documents and nothing but the documents—is merely moving closer and closer to incoherence, chaos, and meaninglessness. That is a dead end for sure. No society will long support a profession that produces arcane trivia and calls it truth.

Fortunately for the profession, historians' practice has been better than their epistemology. Instead of replicating confusion by paraphrasing the totality of relevant and available documents, we have used our sources to discern, support, and reinforce group identities at national, transnational and subnational levels, and, once in a while, to attack or pick apart a group identity to which a school of revisionists has taken a scunner.

If we can now realize that our practice already shows how truths may be discerned at different levels of generality with equal precision simply because different patterns emerge on different time-space scales, then, perhaps, repugnance for world history might diminish and a juster proportion between parochial and ecumenical historiography might begin to emerge. It is our professional duty to move towards ecumenicity, however real the risks may seem to timid and unenterprising minds.

With a more rigorous and reflective epistemology, we might also attain a better historiographical balance between Truth, truths, and myth. Eternal and universal Truth about human behavior is an unattainable goal, however delectable as an ideal. Truths are what historians achieve when they bend their minds as critically and carefully as they can to the task of making their account of public affairs credible as well as intelligible to an audience that shares enough of their particular outlook and assumptions to accept what they say. The result might best be called mythistory perhaps (though I do not expect the term to catch on in professional circles), for the same words that constitute truth for some are, and always will be, myth for others, who inherit or embrace different assumptions and organizing concepts about the world.

This does not mean that there is no difference between one mythistory and another. Some clearly are more adequate to the facts than others. Some embrace more time and space and make sense of a wider variety of human behavior than others. And some, undoubtedly, offer a less treacherous basis for collective action than others. I actually believe that historians' truths, like those of natural science, evolve across the generations, so that versions of the past acceptable today are superior in scope, range, and accuracy to versions available in earlier times. But such evolution is slow, and observable only on an extended time scale, owing to the self-validating character of myth. Effective common action can rest on quite fantastic beliefs. *Credo quia absurdum* may even become a criterion for group membership, requiring initiates to surrender their critical faculties as a sign of full commitment to the common cause. Many sects have prospered on this principle and have served their members well for many generations while doing so.

But faiths, absurd or not, also face a long-run test of survival in a world where not everyone accepts any one set of beliefs and where human beings must interact with external objects and nonhuman forms of life, as well as with one another. Such "foreign relations" impose limits on what any group of people can safely believe and act on, since actions that fail to secure expected and desired results are always costly and often disastrous. Beliefs that mislead action are likely to be amended; too stubborn an adherence to a faith that encourages or demands hurtful behavior is likely to lead to the disintegration and disappearance of any group that refuses to learn from experience.

Thus one may, as an act of faith, believe that our historiographical myth making and myth breaking is bound to cumulate across time, propagating mythistories that fit experience better and allow human survival more often, sustaining in-groups in ways that are less destructive to themselves and to their neighbors than was once the case or is the case today. If so, ever-evolving mythistories will indeed become truer and more adequate to public life, emphasizing the really important aspects of human encounters and omitting irrelevant background noise more efficiently so that men and women will know how to act more wisely than is possible for us today.

This is not a groundless hope. Future historians are unlikely to leave out Blacks and women from any future mythistory of the United States, and we are unlikely to exclude Asians, Africans, and Amerindians from any future mythistory of the world. One hundred years ago this was not so. The scope and range of historiography has widened, and that change looks as irreversible to me as the widening of physics that occurred when Einstein's equations proved capable of explaining phenomena that Newton's could not.

It is far less clear whether in widening the range of our sensibilities and taking a broader range of phenomena into account we also see deeper into the reality we seek to understand. But we may. Anyone who reads historians of the sixteenth or seventeenth centuries and those of our own time will notice a new awareness of social process that we have attained. As one who shares that awareness, I find it impossible not to believe that it represents an advance on older notions that focused attention exclusively, or almost exclusively, on human intentions and individual actions, subject only to God or to a no less inscrutable Fortune, while leaving out the social and material context within which individual actions took place simply because that context was assumed to be uniform and unchanging.

Still, what seems wise and true to me seems irrelevant obfuscation to others. Only time can settle the issue, presumably by outmoding my ideas and my critics' as well. Unalterable and eternal Truth remains like the Kingdom of Heaven, an eschatological hope. Mythistory is what we actually have—a useful instrument for piloting human groups in their encounters with one another and with the natural environment.

To be a truth-seeking mythographer is therefore a high and serious calling, for what a group of people knows and believes about the past channels expectations and affects the decisions on which their lives, their fortunes, and their sacred honor all depend. Formal written histories are not the only shapers of a people's notions about the past; but they are sporadically powerful, since even the most abstract and academic historiographical ideas do trickle down to the level of the commonplace, if they fit both what a people want to hear and what a people need to know well enough to be useful.

As members of society and sharers in the historical process, historians can only expect to be heard if they say what the people around them want to hear—in some degree. They can only be useful if they also tell the people some things they are reluctant to hear—in some degree. Piloting between this Scylla and Charybdis is the art of the serious historian, helping the group he or she addresses and celebrates to survive and prosper in a treacherous and changing world by knowing more about itself and others.

Academic historians have pursued that art with extraordinary energy and considerable success during the past century. May our heirs and successors persevere, and do even better!

# Two

# The Care and Repair of Public Myth

Myth lies at the basis of human society. That is because myths are general statements about the world and its parts, and in particular about nations and other human in-groups, that are believed to be true and then acted on whenever circumstances suggest or require common response. This is mankind's substitute for instinct. It is the unique and characteristic human way of acting together. A people without a full quiver of relevant agreed-upon statements, accepted in advance through education or less formalized acculturation, soon finds itself in deep trouble, for, in the absence of believable myths, coherent public action becomes very difficult to improvise or sustain.

Myths, moreover, are based on faith more than on fact. Their truth is usually proven only by the action

Reprinted by permission of *Foreign Affairs,* Fall 1982. © 1982 by the Council on Foreign Relations, Inc.

they provoke. In 1940, for example, when Hitler had
defeated France, the British public continued to support war against Germany partly because they "knew"
from schoolbook history that in European wars their
country lost all the early battles and always won the
last. This faith, together with a strong sense of the general righteousness of their cause, and fear of what defeat
would bring, made it possible for them to persist in
waging war until myth became fact once more in 1945.

Clearly, without British actions in 1940, World
War II would have followed a far different course. Russian and American resources might never have co-
alesced with Britain's to create the victorious Grand
Alliance of 1945. Germany, in short, might have won.
Yet no merely rational calculation of relative strengths
and military capabilities in June 1940 would have sup-
ported the proposition that Great Britain could expect
to defeat Hitler. Action, irrational in the short run,
proved rational in the longer run. Myth is what
bridged the gap, remaking the reality of June 1940
into the reality of May 1945.

On the other hand, Hitler and his followers, too,
were guided by their own set of myths. But their belief
in Germany's racial superiority, no matter how firmly
embraced and enthusiastically acted upon, brought
only disaster. So belief by itself is not enough. Complex
constraints operate in human affairs, only partially understood even by the wisest. Consequently, human
hopes are never fully realized, and unforeseen side effects continually throw up new problems that redirect
action even in the most routinized situations. It is in
directing and redirecting action that myth comes into

play. Conversely, when actions undertaken in accordance with accepted ideas fail to achieve anything like the expected result, it is time to reconsider the guiding myth, amending or rejecting it as the case may be. As a result of this process, the British national myth survived World War II with little amendment, whereas Germany's suffered a wrenching discontinuity.

Liberalism, Marxism, and the various technocratic ideals of social management that have proliferated so remarkably since World War II all constitute living myth systems, subject to amendment or rejection in the light of results, just as Nazism was. But the feedback between myth and action proceeds smoothly and effectively only when destruction and reconstruction of agreed-upon general statements about the world remain more or less in balance. Discrediting old myths without finding new ones to replace them erodes the basis for common action that once bound those who believed into a public body, capable of acting together.

How can a viable balance between myth making and myth breaking be assured? How can a people know what to believe and how to act? How indeed?

II

The classical liberal recipe for the care and repair of public myth was to rely on a free market in ideas. The United States is committed to this principle by law and to quite extraordinary degree also in practice. By allowing dissenters of any and every stripe a chance to express their views, liberals from the seventeenth century onwards hoped and believed that a kind of natural selection among myths would prevail. When, as is commonly the case, inadequate evidence obstructs fully rational choice, the upshot of action based on tentative or provisional belief would still suffice to permit the people to choose—eventually—what to believe and how to act.

The efficiency of such a free market obviously depends on how long it may take for the process of testing and confirmation—or rejection—to work itself out. In rapidly changing conditions, when more and more dimensions of social life are in motion and become subject to deliberate manipulation, there may not be enough time to test new formulations before they must again be altered to match newer and ever-changing circumstances. Worn-out old myths may then continue to receive lip service, but the spontaneity and force attainable when people truly believe and hope and act in unison will surely seep away.

In some fields, the free market in ideas works very well. This is conspicuously the case in natural science, where myth, tested by action and revised in accordance with results, continues to achieve spectacular success. It may seem whimsical to equate scientific theories with myth, but if one accepts the definition of myth offered at the beginning of this article, surely the shoe fits. Scientific theories *are* statements about the world, believed to be true, and many of them also provide a basis for action, as our extraordinary technology attests. Moreover, no scientist any longer thinks that any actual theory fits reality so closely that revision and amendment will never be needed. No formula, whether mathematical or verbal, is immune from correction. Thus Newton supplanted Aristotle and Descartes, and was in turn corrected by Einstein, whose reign may soon be coming to a close if contemporary physicists succeed in formulating some new synthesis among the strong and weak forces their experiments have discovered.

Continual and fertile interplay between myth making and myth breaking in natural science stands in striking contrast with human affairs, where successful myth making is in short supply. This is not simply because effective social myths must go beyond observed facts. That is just as true in physics and the other natural sciences, where theory regularly runs beyond observation, guides perception and, frequently, directs experiments as well. For it is only where they have a theory to test that scientists can know how to filter out the various background noises that obscure experimental results when such guidance is lacking. Thus fact and theory interact in natural science in almost as strong a way as in human society.

Yet the natural and human worlds are not the same. Their great difference arises from the sensitivity of human behavior to symbolic stimuli. Physicists, after all, need not concern themselves with how particles of matter or energy will react to general statements they make about the world: whereas anyone describing human behavior knows that if what is said seems to be true, it will make a difference in how human beings who believe it will act. Such reflexivity therefore makes social myths different. They are more powerful to create and to destroy what they purport to describe than the formulations of the physicists, whose myths affect only the observation of behavior, not the behavior itself.

In human society, therefore, belief matters most. Evidence supporting belief is largely generated by actions undertaken in accordance with the belief. This is a principle long familiar to students of religion. In Christian terms, faith comes first, works follow. The primacy of faith is equally real for the various civil religions that since the eighteenth century have come to provide the practical basis for nearly all of the world's governments. Democratic elections legitimate governments when enough people believe that periodic elections are the right and proper way to choose who shall rule. For the same reason, divine-right monarchy, caliphal leadership and submission to the Son of Heaven were once effective too. But when assent becomes half-hearted or is actively withheld from such myths, obedience becomes irregular, the predictability of human action diminishes, and the effectiveness of public response to changing conditions begins to erode.

This, it seems to me, is our situation today around the globe. Democratic myths confront the reality of organized private interest groups operating in the interstices of empire building among rival branches of vast and ever-growing governmental bureaucracies. This makes the electoral process increasingly irrelevant to encounters between officials and citizens, even in countries like our own in which elections are not affected by armed intimidation at the polls or limited to candidates approved by a single party.

The audio-visual mass media, by opening a path into

private homes where aspiring candidates may sell
themselves to the voting public, do even more to insu-
late the electoral process from administrative realities.
In the United States a candidate who secures access to
TV has already won half the battle; subliminal empathy
does the rest, slightly affected by the plausibility of
promises to satisfy everyone, dismantle the bureau-
cracy, fight crime and safeguard peace. In other countries political salesmanship takes less extravagant
forms. There, party organizations or governmental officials set more severe limits on access to mass media,
and on programmatic statements attacking constituted
authorities. In poorer lands, where TV screens have not
yet spread into private homes, political campaigns are
still likely to focus in the old-fashioned way on public
meetings and private deals with locally based leaders of
whatever sort—party functionaries, tribal chieftains,
employers, landowners or whoever else matters in getting things done. But everywhere TV acts to under-
mine the electoral process, tending to reduce it to a
popularity contest among tinsel personalities.

Communist countries have restricted the political
impact of mass media by limiting what can be said in
public to a narrow party line. But that policy runs into
difficulties of its own. Apart from a widespread loss of
credibility, the heavy weight of the police regimes that
enforce restriction on public debate blatantly contradicts the anarchic brotherhood promised by Marx's vision of postrevolutionary communism. Consequently,
as revolutions recede in time, the gap between reality
and expectation becomes more difficult to explain
away.

III

Political institutions are therefore not working well on either side of the Iron Curtain. Inherited political faiths are in danger of losing their credibility. The incipient stage of such a change is difficult to recognize or measure accurately; yet withdrawal of belief may suddenly come to matter more than anything else in foreign and domestic affairs. Revolutionary situations, like that which boiled up in Iran in 1979, register the collapse of old belief; but a successful revolution, like every other collective action, must invent or revive its own myths. Stability, predictability, control are otherwise impossible. The body politic cannot endure without agreement on truths that can be used to guide and justify public action.

To be sure, the United States is not in a revolutionary situation. Nonetheless, discrepancies between old myths and current realities are great enough to be troubling. They seem to widen every day, yet serious effort to revise inherited public myths remains largely the province of revivalist sectarians.

In times past, such situations have sometimes given great leaders the opportunity to reshape a nation or to remodel a state in response to a new vision of what was right, proper, and possible. World War II and its aftermath gave this kind of scope to such diverse figures as Charles de Gaulle in France, Konrad Adenauer in Germany, Mao Zedong in China, and Tito in Yugoslavia. Before that, the depression of the 1930s called Franklin D. Roosevelt and Adolf Hitler into action. Maybe our current difficulties will find a similar resolution in one or more of the most deeply affected countries. What is needed is a suitably charismatic figure with a vision of past and future that millions will find so compelling as to make them eager to join in common action to achieve newly articulated purposes.

Nevertheless, though the niche may be empty and waiting, no one can count on its being filled. Great public figures do not arise in a vacuum. They personify and give voice to ideas and ideals already scattered about and accepted by at least some segments of the public that respond to their call. The great leader's role is to put a coalition of new ideas into action, often by dint of overlooking logical discrepancies. When the resulting mix commands enough support to generate effective common action, logical shortcomings scarcely matter. The people who follow the great man's lead have, in effect, revised their mythical system and can therefore persist as an effective public body for as long as the new myths and action based on them continue to yield acceptable results.

But where do political leaders' new ideas come from? Tito and Mao drew on Marxism, Adenauer revivified a Catholic, corporatist tradition that had suffered near total eclipse in Bismarck's Germany, while De Gaulle combined Gallicanism, technocracy, and a personal sense of mission that perhaps derived as much from his name as from anything more tangible. Such traditions are themselves human creations, of course, being largely the work of intellectuals and men of letters, packaged by historians for use in schools and other public places and then transmitted and sustained by educational, religious, and other cultural institutions.

In a time such as ours, when inherited myth systems are in disrepair and no great political leader has yet emerged, historians, political scientists, and other academics who are paid to educate the young and think about matters of public importance ought to feel a special responsibility for proposing alternatives to accepted ideas. Only so can they hope to trigger a successful reorganization of public myths that could command the support of informed and critical minds. To leave the field to ignorant and agitated extremists is dangerous. That, after all, was how Hitler came to power. Yet American historians are doing so today with clear conscience and from the best of motives.

Pursuit of truth has been the overriding ideal of our universities ever since the professionalization of research in academic institutions began about a century ago. Challenging prevailing myths without regard for the costs arising from the disintegration of belief therefore became professors' special calling. Intellectual honesty required as much, and methodological rigor demanded special attention to anything that failed to conform to mythical prescription and expectation.

Hence the enthusiasm for revisionism. Careers have been made and schools of historians have flourished on the strength of their discovery of flaws in received notions about the American nation and its government. By uncovering the sufferings of the poor and oppressed, revisionists discredited older ideas about the unique virtue and perfection of American society. They showed that liberty and democracy did not assure equality after all. Assimilation to a Yankee model of behavior did not guarantee happiness either, even for the most enthusiastic converts from other cultural backgrounds. Still other iconoclasts challenged the belief that foreigners differed from us simply because they had fallen behind the progress of the United States and only needed a little capital and know-how to become as rich, free, and fortunate as Americans were supposed to be.

No one is likely to reaffirm these discredited notions today, even though public rhetoric often assumes the reality of such myths without expressly saying so. Politicians and journalists really have little choice, since suitably revised national and international myths are conspicuous by their absence.

Instead, the main energies of the historical profession have gone into detailed research, often focusing on the experience of groups formerly excluded from historians' attention; i.e., on one or another of the ethnically, sexually, and occupationally oppressed segments of society. Frequently, the effect of such scholarship is to substitute a divisive for a unifying myth, intensifying the special grievances of one group against others.

Truth and intellectual honesty are no doubt served by noting the yawning gaps between democratic ideals and social practice. They would be even better served if historians found it possible to fit their new data and sensibilities into a wider perspective in which weak and strong, oppressor and oppressed would all find a place. In such a history, of course, the things that unite human beings would have to come to the fore. This might even provide a matrix for mutual understanding and more effective public action. Yet macrohistory is commonly deemed unscientific, and this despite the example natural scientists have given of how to react to new, discrepant data by revising theory to embrace old and new in a single formula believed to be true.

The main reason for eschewing macrohistorical synthesis is the mistaken notion that generalization inevitably involves error, while accuracy increases with detail. Getting at the sources and staying close to them seemed a sure way to truth a century ago when academic departments of history were set up. Industrious transcription of dead men's opinions therefore became the hallmark of historical scholarship. It still provides a convenient substitute for thought, despite historical quantifiers and other methodological innovators. Yet an infinitude of new sources, each of them revealing new details, does not automatically increase the stock of historical truth. More data may merely diminish the intelligibility of the past, and, carried to an extreme, the multiplication of facts reduces historical study to triviality.

The truth about foreign affairs, for example, does not reside solely or chiefly in the texts of diplomatic notes filed away in foreign offices. Search of supplementary sources like newspaper files, TV scripts, and private papers will not do much to remedy the defects of diplomatic history based on faithful transcription and comparison of official documents. The reason is that all such research assumes that the situations within which human beings act are obvious and unchanging, so that only operational details that passed through the consciousness of the actors at the time need to be attended to.

But this is not the case, and historians actually know

better. States are not eternal; nations emerge and pass
away. Alterations in communication nets change the
way governments and peoples interact, and patterns of
power transform themselves all the time in ways of
which contemporaries are only dimly aware. Yet
changes of this kind commonly matter more for understanding what happened than anything that can be discovered by consulting additional past opinions as
recorded in sources hitherto unexplored. Indus-
triousness in archives may merely obstruct vision of the
larger patterns whose evolution matters far more than
new details of particular transactions.

To move from detail to perception of larger patterns
is not achieved by accumulating more and more instances. Appropriate concepts are needed. Each change
of scale requires its own vocabulary to direct attention
to the critical thresholds and variables. Finding the
right things to lump together and the right words to
focus attention on critical transitions is the special work
of human intelligence—whether applied to history or
to everyday encounters with the world. Nearly everything is done for us by the language we inherit that
generalizes and organizes the flow of sensory experience
with every noun and verb we employ. But myth makers
and myth breakers are entrusted with the task of ad-
justing and improving received ways of understanding
and reacting to the world. As such, they are supposed
to think more persistently and perspicaciously than
others, making whatever change may be needed in inherited words and concepts so as to take account of new
experience.

Finding the right vocabulary to focus attention efficiently is a difficult matter. The history of human thought records some of the more successful efforts that have been made. As a result of centuries of struggle to come to grips with the complexity of things, we now have many separate sciences, each with its own vocabulary. These actually describe the same reality at different levels of generalization. Thus, for example, no one doubts that atoms, molecules, cells and organisms simultaneously occupy terrestrial landscapes, and we have appropriate sciences for each. We also know that complicated ecological relationships exist among the separate organisms and populations of organisms that share any particular part of the earth. However complicated the relation may be across these diverse levels of organization, it is not the case that small patterns are automatically truer than large patterns, or that error inheres in a description of the ecosystem but is absent from formulas that apply to atomic interactions. Indeterminacy extends to the atomic and subatomic level too, as twentieth-century physicists agree.

Historians, however, through their idolization of written sources, have commonly allowed themselves to wallow in detail, while refusing to think about the larger patterns of the past which cannot be discovered by consulting documentary sources. They have consequently undermined inherited myths that attempted to make the past useful by describing large-scale patterns, without feeling any responsibility for replacing decrepit old myths with modified and corrected general statements that might provide a better basis for public action.

## IV

If historians persist in dodging the important questions of our age in this fashion, others are sure to step into the breach by offering the necessary mythical answers to human needs. The question then becomes what groupings will take form and gather strength around such myths. So far, sectarian fissiparousness seems the dominant trend. Religious syncretism and revival, whether Muslim, Christian, Hindu, or Buddhist, achieve success largely by cutting true believers off from the corruptions of civil society around them. Secular forms of sectarianism seem at a low ebb by comparison, thanks to the wearing out of both the Freudian and the Marxist faiths.

Tides in myth making and myth breaking are, of course, unpredictable and have often taken sudden, surprising turns. Recent events in Iran remind us of how precariously old and new systems of ideas coexist. Yet I, for one, am not prepared to abandon a secular and ecumenical faith in the power of human minds to decipher the world.

Several points seem clear to me. One is that troubling encounters with strangers constitute the principal motor of change within human societies. Ecumenical world history ought therefore to be specially sensitive to traces of past cultural interactions. This has the immediate effect of escaping the Europe-centered bias we have inherited, for any plausible view of the human adventure on earth quickly discovers that the dominance of European civilization is a matter of recent centuries. European expansion since 1500, indeed, appears to be analogous to what happened before when Middle Eastern, Mediterranean, Indian, and Chinese civilizations each in turn attained skills superior to those known elsewhere, and for a few centuries were therefore able to influence others within the interacting circle of the Old World.

Whoever admired or feared the skills in question set out to acquire them or else sought to strengthen local society against their threat. Either way change resulted, often of a far-reaching kind. Comparable but less well-established patterns of cultural efflorescence and outward flow can be discerned among pre-Columbian Amerindians. African history, too, begins to become intelligible—though still dimly—in terms of diffusion of skills of the kind recorded more fully by the literate civilizations of Eurasia.

A second obvious proposition is that the national history of the United States fits into the pattern of world history not as an exception but as a part. More specifically, the rise of the United States was an important segment of the global phenomenon of European expansion that dominated most of the earth from shortly before 1500 to shortly after 1900. The U.S.S.R., too, is a monument to the same process, having been built by pioneers who moved eastward and overland rather than westward and overseas as in the case of the United States. This geographical difference had important consequences for the fashion in which the repertory of European skills and institutions was altered and adapted on the two frontiers. But such differences ought not to obscure what was common to all European

frontier societies, East and West, and also in such diversified places as South Africa, Australasia, and South
America.

Placing our national experience within the panorama
of world history will require us to give up both the
original Puritan vision of creating a "city on the hill"
uniquely pleasing to God, and its variously secularized
versions that continue to dominate our national self-
image. Manifest Destiny, translated into an aggressive,
hard-nosed pursuit of national advantage in the tradition of Theodore Roosevelt and his successors, is as
unsatisfactory a guide to action today as is the univer-
salistic legal-moralism associated with Woodrow
Wilson and his political heirs. Limits to our national
power need to be recognized more clearly than either of
these traditions admits. The plain fact is that the
wealth and power of the United States vis-à-vis the rest
of the world have diminished since 1945, and we must
get used to this elemental fact. The best way to start is
to recognize that the American way of life is no more
than one variation among many to which humanity
adheres.

This need not diminish personal and collective attachment to inherited values and institutions. Recognition of humanity's cultural pluralism might, indeed,
allow us to react more intelligently to encounters with
other peoples than is likely to happen when we are either aggrieved and surprised by their persistent, willful
differences from us, or else remain self-righteously im-
pervious to the possibility of learning something useful
from people who diverge from us in enduring, conspicuous ways.

Finally, it seems no less evident that currents of cultural interaction have, since 1914, begun to run in new directions from those that dominated the world during the preceding four centuries. How to understand the contemporary scene requires more detachment from everyday events than we can easily achieve. For a while after World War II, the bipolar diplomatic pattern of the cold war seemed to ratify the existence of rival and opposing Soviet-U.S. spheres of influence. But Japan's economic rise, together with heartfelt Third World aspiration toward a more perfect emancipation from imperial tutelage, and complex cross-currents within old Europe that extend, sometimes, to Russian and American societies as well, makes that simple bipolarity now seem inadequate in spite of President Reagan's efforts to make it the key to all else.

Perspective arising from the course of future events may be necessary before observers can discern the pattern of our time as clearly as we can recognize past patterns of interaction among the peoples and cultures of the earth. Nonetheless, seeing contemporary foreign affairs as a continuation of longstanding processes of cultural encounter will surely teach us not to expect the various peoples of the earth to wish to be like us any more than we wish to be like them. It should teach us also to expect local variation in the expression of even the most universal human aspirations. The fact that nearly everyone prefers wealth and power to poverty and helplessness does not therefore assure any uniformity in the way different peoples will choose to pursue the common goal. Nor are material goods everything. Beauty and holiness are also widely disseminated ideals, and the desire for membership in a supportive community of comrades is an even more universal and, often, passionate desire.


## V

The most problematic of all these human aspirations is how to define the limits of comradeship. This, indeed, is where humanity's myth-making and myth-destroying capacity comes elementally and directly into play by defining the boundary between "us" and "them." Broadly inclusive public identities, if believed and acted on, tend to relax tensions among strangers and can allow people of diverse habits and outlook to coexist more or less peacefully. Narrowed in-group loyalties, on the other hand, divide humanity into potentially or actually hostile groupings.

The choice is awkward because advantages do not lie wholly on one side. Sectarian groups, their faces set firmly against the larger world, are far more supportive of their members than variegated, pluralistic societies can be. Nations, for the same reason, provide their citizens with more vibrant public identities than transnational and global organizations will ever be able to do. What humanity needs is balance between a range of competing identities. A single individual ought to be able to be a citizen of the world and hold membership in a series of other, less inclusive in-groups simultaneously, all without suffering irreconcilable conflict among competing loyalties. But that could only occur if conventional limits to jurisdiction somehow stabilized relationships among all the multitude of possible in-groups. Such stability has perhaps been approached in times past when some territorially vast empire brought order of a kind to parts of the globe, but it is no recipe for our foreseeable future.

Instead we must do the best we can to survive in a world full of conflict by creating and sustaining the most effective public identities of which we are capable. Cultural diversity is and always has been characteristic of the human species. No sensible person would wish or expect to see uniformity instead. Ordering diversity is, nonetheless, difficult. Violence played a large role in times past, by defining geographic boundaries and modes of interaction among diverse communities. Violence is sure to remain among us, heirs as we are of hunting bands that became the most skillful of all predators. But wisdom can sometimes restrain violence, or channel it into less damaging forms of behavior than preparation for atomic war.

Apart from the practical value which serious myth making aspires to, the reality of world society in our day constitutes an intellectual challenge that can be met only by rising to the grandest mythical plane of which we are capable. Only so can the world we live in become intelligible. Inherited ideas—whether dating back to pagan Greece, Christian Europe, 1776 or 1848—are simply inadequate, and there is no use pretending otherwise. There is still less sense in pretending that all we need is more detail. What we need is an intelligible world, and to make the world intelligible, generalization is necessary. Our academic historians have not done well in providing such generalizations of late. Thoughtful men of letters ought therefore to try.

# Three

## *The Rise of the West as a Long-Term Process*

Twenty-one years ago I ended my principal work with the words:

> "The Rise of the West" may serve as a shorthand description of the upshot of the history of the human community to date. The rise of the west as intended by the title and meaning of this book is only accelerated when one or another Asian or African people throws off European administration by making western techniques, attitudes, and ideas sufficiently their own to permit them to do so.[1]

Prepared for the "Conference on Civilization and the Civilizing Process," University of Bielefeld Center for Interdisciplinary Research, 15–17 June 1984, and published as "De opkomst van het westen als een langetermijn ontwikkeling" in *Sociologisch Tijdschrift* 11, Oct. 1984.
1. William H. McNeill, *The Rise of the West: A History of the Human Community* (Chicago: University of Chicago Press, 1963), p. 807.

This seems as obvious today as it did then. Emergence of a new style of civilization and of a new geographical center capable of influencing the rest of the earth will take time, if, indeed, it occurs at all; and human lives are far too short for us to count on seeing any such shift come to pass.

Nevertheless, from the vantage point of an individual lifetime and of the concepts available in that lifetime, as historians we must try to understand what happened in order to reduce the multiplex simultaneity of events as experienced by millions of diverse human beings to the slender proportions of grammatical discourse. Only by knowing what to leave out, what not to pay attention to, can such a feat be achieved. And only by accepting and then acting on a theory of social process can historians expect to have a criterion of relevance to guide them amidst the confusing plethora of data potentially available to their researches.

Selective transcription of what happened to be recorded in times past is not enough, even though many historians seem still to believe that ready-made truths about the past are to be found in primary sources, and need only to be transferred from the obscurity of the archives to the obscurity of learned discourse by a simple act of copying. But a collection of all the primary sources in the world would not record the whole truth. Experience is too multifaceted, too infinite for that. Whatever gets written down is itself an interpretation and drastic simplification of what actually went on. Moreover, what really happened can only be partly known at the time, since men are always ignorant of the full significance of their acts. Only subsequently—

sometimes many centuries subsequently—can some meanings of particular acts such as the Crucifixion or Charlemagne's coronation at Rome become apparent.

There is also a statistical side to behavior that remains aloof from, and largely independent of, individual intention and consciousness. Economists have long been aware that individual decisions to buy and sell add up to boom-and-bust rhythms of economic exchange—rhythms which no one plans but which nevertheless assert themselves even when no one desires it. Population dynamics exhibit other, less precise rhythms of unintended growth and decline. Cultural creativity, too, rises and falls in ways no one understands. These and other patterns of behavior can often be recognized in retrospect, whereas contemporaneous observation of even the most familiar statistical patterns remains very difficult. Sophisticated economic indicators, for example, although devised by statisticians acutely aware of boom-and-bust patterns, are still not fully capable of registering the ups and downs of the marketplace as experienced in 1984.

A further complication arises from the fact that when a population learns to expect some sort of statistical fluctuation that seriously affects individual lives, then behavior alters in anticipation of that fluctuation. Sometimes the effect is to exaggerate the phenomenon, as in the case of old-fashioned runs on banks; sometimes the effect is to damp back the expected fluctuation, as in the case of deposit insurance.

In either case, consciousness intervenes, directing conduct in the light of human concepts about the world and what is likely to happen in it. So changing ideas

enter into and affect social behavior, social behavior affects ideas, and all the while innumerable human
beings are acting and thinking and feeling variably
from moment to moment, and recording almost nothing of their ever-changing state of being and consciousness. Yet surely it is the flickering flame of
human consciousnesses that constitutes experiential reality—a reality buried and forgotten by each one of us
moment by moment throughout our lives. Only fragments are ever written down or recorded in some other
fashion; and such records are themselves selective,
coded and interpreted representations of the reality, far
removed from what actually happened, even in a single
human mind.

If one takes a rigorous epistemological stance, therefore, writing a history of what really happened quickly
becomes impossible. All we have is words and, perhaps, recorded visual images. Words are themselves
embedded in languages; and languages are social products, permitting groups of human beings to communicate and thus concert their activities in common. The
main function of words is to generalize experience, imposing categories and classes upon the flow of sensory
inputs, and thereby allowing us to recognize useful objects, e.g., "table," in innumerable and sharply different encounters with things. Beyond that, our words
create the social world we live in to a very large degree,
permitting us to recognize and respond appropriately
to a policeman, a professor, a foreigner, or a fellow citizen as the case may be. Agreed-upon categories and
classes of encounters with other human beings give
meaning and direction to individual lives, tie us into
human society, and constrain us to relatively predict-

able acts. Predictable individual acts become customs and mores in the aggregate. They harden into law in complicated societies when reduced to writing and enforced by kings and magistrates.

The survival value of such artifice is obvious. Predictable social behavior is safer and more comfortable for all concerned and far more effective, inasmuch as under a regime of law and custom coordinated effort on the part of large numbers of individuals makes it possible to accomplish tasks otherwise beyond human capacity. Symbolic discourse thus gives human beings their extraordinary capacity to transform the natural world by collective effort. It is, indeed, what makes us human.

Historians are principally concerned with this semeiological level of human interaction, and since words are what mainly sustain such behavior, it is fitting and proper that historians should also rely upon words, interpreted from sources and strung together into discourse, to find meaning in the past.

But just as words, and concepts embodied in words, create the social universe within which humans live and move and have their being, so also historians must choose a set of words and concepts with which to give meaning to the past. To begin with, the obvious resort was to employ concepts at work in whatever society the historian happened to be a part of. This meant projecting local ethnocentric views of human conduct on aliens and ancestors among whom very different norms sometimes prevailed. History under such circumstances was Procrustean. Discrepant behavior was either lopped from the historical record, or else exaggerated to show that those who behaved in such outrageous fashion were not really human. By writing local and chronologically

restricted histories, puzzling incommensurabilities between expectation and recorded events could be mini-
mized, of course; and by recording the triumphs of
local ideals in action, historians could do much to sta-
bilize group behavior and define norms for subsequent
generations. Such local ethnocentric histories could
thereby carry the stabilization of behavior one step beyond what law could do, making conformity voluntary
and enthusiastic and, perchance, more efficient and effective for being freely entered upon.

The role of defining and strengthening in-groups by
codifying a flattering version of each group's particular
past is, indeed, the principal social function that historians played, and continue to play in the contemporary
world as much as in antiquity. For this purpose a historian needs only to master the language of the group
whose existence and shared experiences he chooses to
celebrate, though good historians and those who attained greatness regularly went beyond any given in-
group's universe of discourse to consider the environing
society as well. Thereby they tended to modulate the
naive egoism and self-righteousness that all in-groups
display ("us" vs. "them") by recognizing the shared
humanity that runs beyond in-group boundaries and
connects each group with other human beings. Such
ecumenical histories are needed to prepare any given
group for the buffetings of the larger world, in which
others do not share its peculiarities and commonly dis-
trust or dislike what loyal members of the in-group
most delight in.

The familiar historiographic record shows this process in action clearly enough. In the nineteenth cen-

tury, historians constructed glorious national histories for the various states of Europe and the Europeanized parts of the earth. Since World War II, a parallel enterprise is in train in newly independent states, but in the heartlands of the western world the most vigorous historical writing focuses upon experience at the private level—familial and demographic changes—or on variously oppressed subnational groups: peasants, workers, women, the insane, etc. A smaller company of historians went the other way, inquiring into transnational themes and even aiming at world history in its entirety.

These new currents of historiography both reflect and reinforce the emergence of new group consciousnesses that in some degree challenge the national state. In writing the new histories, research scholars thus contribute to the continuing evolution of their societies, changing human consciousness in some slight degree by affecting the flow of messages that sustains and creates the human groupings within which each of us lives.

The shift towards subnational and transnational historiography remains far too weak to challenge the centrality of national-scale history writing. Yet within each of the leading national professional communities, the broadening of range inherent in these departures from the national frame puts considerable strain on the commonality of the historiographical enterprise. Historians who stick close to the primary sources and adorn their pages with ample quotes to demonstrate the accuracy of what they have discovered, do not seem to be doing the same thing that historians of civilizations and millennia are doing when they write world history.

The principal reason is that microhistorians can often move comfortably within a single, more or less coherent universe of discourse simply by reproducing words and concepts familiar among those whose history they write. Professional macrohistorians, seeking to deal with human beings who espoused very divergent ideas about the world and how to behave in it, can scarcely do the same. Yet they cannot entirely abandon inherited language and concepts either. What they need is a specialized terminology, safely embedded in a flexible mother tongue, which will somehow be capable of ordering the experience of human beings in general, despite all the cultural diversity that human minds have elaborated across millennia.

Such a vocabulary has been slow to arise, and no one, I think, will claim that it has yet evolved a satisfactory scope and precision. Yet a real beginning has been made, and in making it macrohistorians tend to pull apart from the company of microhistorians who study in-groups close to themselves in time and sympathy, whose local language therefore seems appropriate and adequate for recording the sufferings and triumphs that impinged on the consciousness of at least some individuals within the group, and which happened then to be written down. Such history, directly transcribed from primary sources though it be, remains inherently partial, and commonly abdicates any serious effort to locate the group experience within those larger social processes that are so dear to the heart of the macrohistorian, but which remain absent from the consciousness of human beings as they actually experience life.

Here lurks the principal professional discrepancy of our age. The central notion for all varieties of macrohistory is that of a social process (or processes) acting largely in independence of human awareness and so, by definition, not to be found recorded and awaiting discovery in some primary source. Yet it is worth pointing out that scale is not the decisive factor separating the two schools. Rather it is the difference between those willing to remain safely encapsulated within a given group's universe of discourse and those seeking somehow to transcend cultural boundaries. Ancient and medieval historians as well as historians of exotic lands regularly resort to terms and explanations that are far removed from the *ipsissima verba* of their sources, no matter how minute the subject of their inquiry. That, indeed, is what source criticism, the pride of our nineteenth-century predecessors, meant.

But when world historians come along and blithely use terms that distance them from the common assumptions of their own time and place as well as from those that governed the lives of people in the past, the validity of their procedures becomes questionable in a new way. Critical historians commonly use modern language to bring the objects of their study into conformity with our local, contemporary expectation and views of human probability. World historians are trying to perform a feat of intellectual prestidigitation, subordinating their own local social universe along with everyone else's to patterns and processes of which those concerned remain largely or entirely unaware. Yet insofar as they succeed and are attended to, the society around them will, in the changeable, intelligent human fashion, begin to alter its behavior in the light of their new awareness.

How can historians or anyone else pretend to hold themselves apart from the social, intellectual, and cultural context in which they find themselves? How indeed? Frankly, I do not think it is possible, although one assuredly can stretch and adjust inherited concepts and expectations in ways that transcend at least some local biases. In particular, one may make room for human cultural diversity by devaluing the accuracy and adequacy of ordinary human consciousness, and supposing instead that human experience fits into some sort of newly invoked, precariously discerned "social process." Such tricks, played on the distant and the dead, are quite safe; but when the validity of a living group's self-consciousness and professed goals are called into question, the historian is likely to appear both arrogant and inaccurate to all who hold to local patterns of belief and to conduct based on that belief.

Why then does "social process" hold such fascination for macrohistorians? The concept, it seems to me, claims our intellectual allegiance because it recognizes and allows for what men have always known: that what happens never completely conforms to advance expectations, while deliberately undertaken actions often provoke side effects that appall and dismay those who have to cope with the situation. In all traditional societies, wise men explained such discrepancies by invoking outside wills, usually the will of God or gods, or some lesser spirit. Sometimes miscarriage of an enterprise was blamed on the malevolence of mere human beings—the enemy, or some witch or traitor to the cause. But serious historians from Herodotus to Ranke and Toynbee explained the course of history, with all its surprises, by recognizing divine will acting among men in a fashion accessible only to faith.

I should stress that this view of the human condition is logically proof against criticism if one grants the premise of God's existence and His power to will and thereby govern the universe. Yet ever since antiquity, and more especially since the eighteenth century, many reflective persons have found the divine inscrutability an unsatisfactory resting place for historical explanation. They therefore developed the notion of social process as a surrogate. So far, I must say, the inscrutability of social process is not notably less than the inscrutability of Providence that it supplants. Yet it is to the anatomy of social process and its better understanding that I have devoted my professional career, and not without some sense of satisfaction and accomplishment. Let me try to sketch my view of what it is that I and other macrohistorians are trying to do, and how we got where we are in anatomizing this surrogate deity of ours—social process.

The starting point, I suppose, was the vision of a world machine generated by Galileo, Descartes, and Newton. If matter and energy behaved according to simple rules, might not human behavior be similarly lawful? Adam Smith's unseen hand, utilizing individual selfishness to enrich society, offers an early example of this line of thought, but it was only in the lee of the French Revolution, and in the minds of Hegel and Marx, that the concept of social process became fully generalized. Yet the realization of freedom in the

Prussian state that Hegel discerned in the record of history, and Karl Marx's dialectic of class struggle, were both firmly rooted in European historical patterns and left no real room for the non-European majority of humankind. Marx's slave-serf-wage worker sequence simply will not fit Asian, African, and Amerindian societies any more than Hegel's Prussian freedom did. This, it seems to me, was the crippling deficiency of these early efforts at anatomizing social process in history.

Escape from hampering ethnocentrism came from two distinct directions. One was anthropological. With the establishment of European dominion over most of Africa and Oceania, a great variety of peoples came to the attention of European scholars, including many who seemed primitive to the anthropologists who studied them. Initial efforts to discover some simple evolutionary pattern among the earth's peoples went out of fashion—at least in the United States—in the 1920s. Instead, anthropologists undertook to study what they could see and handle directly; i.e., material objects, customs, and folkways of Amerindian tribes and of some other isolated (mostly Oceanian) peoples.

Field anthropologists of the 1920s and 1930s were usually romantics. They hoped to find meaning and coherence among primitives in contrast to a growing incoherence in their own urban American moral universe, where the truth of inherited values was no longer obvious. What they sought they found. Anthropologists accordingly reported that the remote communities they had studied exhibited firm and coherent patterns of culture, varying indefinitely from one another, but each valid and livable in its own terms.

The more intellectually ambitious sought larger patterns of coherence. Clark Wissler, for example, studied patterns of diffusion among Plains Indians by plotting the geographical distribution of particular items of material culture. The resulting isobars could be convincingly interpreted as demonstrating a process of cultural diffusion northward from Mexico. Scientific as against merely speculative historical reconstruction of patterns of primitive life could thus be achieved, or so its proponents believed.

Another school of anthropology was less interested in historical reconstruction than in systematic description. For these scholars, time was trivial. What they wanted was an accurate typology of human society. Thus, the spectrum extending from civilized to folk society that Robert Redfield constructed was in principle applicable anywhere, any time. Since the characteristics of his two ideal types of society were abstract and general, they could be used to situate any particular society somewhere between the two theoretical extremes.

Contemporary American and European society, it must be admitted, figured near the extreme, "civilized" end of Redfield's spectrum, being more secular, more diverse and incoherent, and more changeable than others. But such traits were costly. The enhanced power and wealth that civilized populations undoubtedly enjoyed had, it appeared, been won at a heavy psychological price—alienation, anomie, and personal isolation. The blithe assumption of older generations, to the effect that all humanity ought and would aspire to imitate the American and European example, no longer seemed plausible. Our civilization, as exhibited by the western world of the 1930s, seemed an ambiguous good at best.

While this anthropological tradition flowered in the United States, a rather different line of development took place in Europe, rooted in the uneasy relationship between Frenchmen and Germans. In the late eighteenth century, a heartfelt wish to assert independence from French cultural models led Johann Gottfried von Herder and other Germans to emphasize language as the natural vehicle for the expression of a people's soul. Different languages therefore created different cultures, each with a claim to unique value. Deference to older, more polished, but also more decrepit civilizations, such as that of France, was thus misguided. Germans (and Slavs!) should instead rely on their own folk spirit and shape their own culture in the hope and expectation of surpassing the French in due season, when natural rhythms of growth and senescence made themselves manifest.

This notion of plural cultures, each with a life of its own and predictable rhythms of growth and decay, was expanded to embrace the globe by Oswald Spengler. Then Arnold J. Toynbee picked up the idea, partly from Spengler's pages and partly from his personal encounter with Balkan peoples and their alien ways as expressed in savage massacres between 1912 and 1922. Civilization, which had been singular in French and English usage before World War I, thus became plural; and relations between separate civilizations became, at least potentially, subject to the sorts of analysis that American anthropologists had used to discern relationships among Amerindian tribes on the high plains.

This, in a nutshell, was my agenda in 1954 when I set out to write a world history. In effect I proposed to turn Spengler and Toynbee on their heads, as Marx claimed to have done to Hegel; for oddly, it seemed to me in view of the record, both Spengler and Toynbee asserted that separate civilizations borrowed nothing of importance from one another, but instead lived out their separate lives in accord with some inner organismic life-force or state of mind. Material borrowings, however obvious, seemed trivial to these pioneers of global history, for they were interested in what Toynbee called "the state of the soul" among those who shared in each of the great civilizations and disdained everyday material objects of the kind anthropologists had found so entrancing.

My approach, influenced by the anthropologists, assumed that borrowing was the normal human reaction to an encounter with strangers possessing superior skills. Even when borrowing proved impractical or undesirable, adjustment of existing ways of life might become necessary to protect against the seduction or threat inherent in contact with the strangers' apparent superiority. Such encounters thus appeared to me to be the principal motor of social change within civilized and simpler societies alike. A world history should, accordingly, focus special attention on modes of transport and the evidences of contact between different and divergent forms of society that such transport allowed.

Let me expatiate a little on my assumptions about

the process of social change, before summarizing the conclusions I came to and reflecting briefly on changes in my outlook that have occurred since 1963, when my book was published.

Social life, like physical change, requires some sort of force to set it in motion. Since contact with strangers provides the principal impetus to change, isolated human communities can be expected to settle down to a fixed routine by developing customs and techniques to meet all the standard situations of human life. In such a community, everyone would always know what to do without having to think about it. This, I believe, was the normal condition of hunters and gatherers throughout prehistoric times. Presumably inherited aptitudes in some profound sense fit us for such tightly knit, unthinking sociality.

Counteracting this normal stability is human inventiveness. This stems from play—play of the hand and eye and of the mind's eye, rearranging objects or words and symbols in some new fashion. Invention can be made for the fun of it and, occasionally, to see how some new scheme might work in practice. But inventions that catch on are more often associated with a time of crisis when some unusual circumstance imposes frustration on individuals or on an entire community. In extreme cases, when customary responses fail to achieve expected and desired results, random behavior sets in—frantic and usually destructive. Yet once in a while a new workable pattern emerges from crisis situations—something that allows individuals or the community in question to exploit a new ecological niche, to relieve extreme situations by effective prophylactic action, or in some other way to improve chances of survival.

For a long time, probably, the principal crises human communities faced were ecological, and a long succession of inventions—tools, weapons, fire, clothing, and artifical shelter suited to all the variations of the earth's climate—resulted. But when almost all the habitable surface of the earth had been occupied; i.e., by about 8000 B.C., contacts with other human communities began to become more important in provoking innovation. This was due to skill differentiation that set in as new ways of getting enough to eat became more and more important. Hunting and gathering— the initial mode of human existence—was gradually supplemented by rearrangement of natural landscapes through human action, so as to increase the number of animals and plants suited for human food. As this occurred, varying skills for producing larger food supplies arose. Some could be applied only in very specialized places, such as river flood plains, while others were applicable across much wider areas—slash-and-burn cultivation, for example, works well on almost any forested ground.

As varying skills diversified the life-styles of human groups, borrowing supplanted invention as the principal impetus to social change. After all, it is far easier to copy someone else than to work things out for oneself, and results are likely to seem far surer in advance. Contact between divergent human communities thereupon assumed the central role in provoking social change that it continued to occupy throughout succeeding generations down to our own time, when, all too obviously, the major impulse to continued technical change arises from the US-USSR arms race.

The process of borrowing and change went into higher gear after 3000 B.C., when civilizations first started. These were societies favored by an especially productive agriculture that began to sustain occupational specialists whose skills, through repeated exercise, quickly came to surpass those of ordinary, unspecialized food producers. Internal differentiation introduced serious friction to the body politic of civilized societies—Marx's class struggle. It also sustained higher skills, and the enhanced wealth and power such skills could create.

Superior wealth and power in its turn provoked envy and imitation among neighbors and neighbors' neighbors across hundreds of miles. The result was to set in motion complex patterns of invasion and conquest, of acculturation and of deliberate reinforcement of cultural differences in order to protect local practices from external threat. Overall, we see a whirl of cultural change, increasingly massive as time went by and as more and more distant human communities became involved in the process of civilized expansion—for that was the upshot of all that happened.

Civilization expanded because most people most of the time preferred the enhanced wealth and power that civilized patterns of society conferred, and this despite the inequalities of status and income that specialization involved, and the surrender or modification of old ways and egalitarian ideals that incorporation into civilized societies required. The result was that by 2000 B.C., the diffusion of civilized skills was altering human behavior all across the Old World, from the valley of the Yellow River to Mesopotamia, and from Mesopotamia to India and the Mediterranean shores. Shortly before the Christian era, contacts across Asia became institutionalized in the form of caravans that traversed the entire continent on a regular basis. Interaction among the civilizations of Eurasia intensified accordingly. Then, after A.D. 1500, the hitherto independent (and less skilled) Amerindian system of interacting civilizations was incorporated abruptly into the Old World ecumenical system.

Nevertheless, local societies did not always crumble after contact with civilized polities or lose inherited patterns of culture just because they found themselves compelled or seduced into reacting to strangers with skills superior to their own. Selective borrowing was often possible. Such borrowings might fit into existing patterns of society with no very great difficulty, or might, on the other hand, precipitate a series of unanticipated further adjustments and readjustments. Severe and drastic periods of change brought about in this fashion tended to come in waves. Periods of unusually rapid change gave place to periods of comparative stability in an irregular and unpredictable rhythm. But civilized communities, being located at the primary foci of the whole accelerated cultural process, were never long at rest. Internal strains and external threats were perennial, and never allowed cessation of significant social change in each of the major civilized centers of the world.

Recurrent rhythms of state rivalry leading to unification of large territories under a single ruler are clearly

perceptible within each of the civilizations of Eurasia
and also of America. This was Toynbee's great discovery. But such empires were never stable for long; and
eras of collapse and invasion not infrequently provoked
fundamental new departures, thanks to fresh contacts,
desperate invention, and eager borrowings by populations no longer sure that their inherited skills and at-
titudes were adequate.

This, in summary, was the social theory I used to
make the writing of a world history possible. I simply
set out to identify in any given age where the center of
highest skills was located. By describing them and then
asking how neighboring peoples reacted to such
achievements, a comprehensible structure for successive
periods of world history emerges, each distinguished
from its predecessors and successors by a pattern of cultural flow outward from a dominant metropolitan center. I need not rehearse details. Suffice it to say that I
fixed upon successive efflorescences, beginning in
Mesopotamia (3000–1800 B.C.), then in a cosmopolitan Middle East, taken as a whole (1800–500 B.C.).
Next the Aegean basin and Mediterranean shorelands
rose to primacy (500 B.C.–A.D. 200). Then it was India's turn (200–600), only to be succeeded by the
Moslems, based in a reintegrated Middle East (600–
1000). In the most recent millennium, world leadership oscillated toward the extremes: first the Far East
(1000–1500), and most recently the Far West (1500–
1950).

Each era of efflorescence, after the first, involved a
preparatory period of large-scale borrowing from more
accomplished cultures—usually from the civilized cen-

ter dominant in the immediately preceeding era. But such borrowed elements entered a distinct institutional and cultural setting, and thereby characteristically attained new scope and importance—often of a far-going kind. (Consider Europe's use of Chinese gunpowder and printing!) This, along with a continuing flow of new invention, and drastic efforts to accommodate old and new in some supportable symbiosis, was what provoked each period of efflorescence and allowed some new region to forge ahead of other peoples in defining a new, powerful, and attractive way of life.

Such perspective makes Europe's recent global dominion simply the most recent example of a recurrent phenomenon. To be sure, intensified communications and cheapened transportation meant that the impact of European civilization on other parts of the earth was much more severe than anything that had ever happened before. Local autonomy of the kind that used to prevail, as between each of the principal Eurasian civilizations, is now clearly diminished by the density of contemporary communication. Perhaps the processes that used to reward a clustering of high skills within a relatively small geographical compass will be modified by instantaneous electronic signals. But as long as cities form and governments govern, it seems likely that centers of cultural dominance and cultural slopes toward provincial backwardness will continue to exist among us. If so, the long-standing pattern of sporadic shift in the location of dominating metropolitan centers may be expected to continue to manifest itself among the great cities and civilizations that share the management of human affairs today, as in times past.

Since 1963, when my book was published, two modifications of my views have achieved a modicum of precision. First of all, I am more conscious of the slow emergence of our contemporary ecumenical society than I used to be, and less satisfied by the notion of separate civilizations as the key concept of world history. In particular, the autonomy I attributed to the major Eurasian civilizations until 1850 ought to be modified by recognizing an emergent ecumenical cosmopolitanism, starting with the establishment of caravan connections before the time of Christ. Ecumenical cosmopolitanism attained intensified significance from A.D. 1000, when China and western Europe alike began to participate in a sophisticated world market far more intensively than before. It looks to me now as though the ancient history of Mesopotamia, Egypt, and the Indus civilizations, which subsequently merged into a cosmopolitan Middle Eastern civilization, was in effect recapitulated on an enlarged geographic scale after 500 B.C., the principal actors having become China, India, and Europe, in addition to the Middle East.

This way of thinking about the history of the world emphasizes communication even more than I did before, and reduces the separateness of the world's civilizations more drastically than I did when writing *The Rise of the West*. But communication is what makes us human, and civilization is no more than a shorthand summation for myriads of messages exchanged among large populations and uniting them in fundamental beliefs and expectations. Changing traffic patterns define changing social groups, and there is nothing sacred about "civilization" as a unit. Historic civilizations were, perhaps, no more than a register of the dimensions of communications systems based on writing (sacred scriptures above all) in combination with animal transport and sailing ships. New modes of communication may therefore be expected to create new patterns of human association, and the old civilizational building blocks may, in time, erode away. Who knows?

The second considerable modification of my views is this: I now believe that human culture is itself set in an ecological context that evolves in partial independence of cultural developments. This is notably the case with infectious diseases, as I argued in *Plagues and Peoples* (1976). Climate is another significant variable which I had previously overlooked. Deforestation, pollution, and other large-scale changes in the ecosystem may yet prove to be a third. The ever-changing ratios between human numbers and resources, as currently available for the maintenance of human life, in accordance with a particular technological and social structure, constitute still a fourth at least quasi-ecological limit upon human affairs.

More generally, human life and society, it seems to me, can best be understood as resting within a hierarchy of equilibria, each of which is itself dynamic and susceptible to unending and occasionally to catastrophic change. First is the physiological—an equilibrium among molecules. Next is ecological—an equilibrium among organisms. Last is semeiological—an equilibrium among symbols. Human cultural behavior operates at the level of symbols, of course; and how we behave from day to day depends primarily on symbolic messages in and messages out that define our consciousness. The symbolic world is complicated enough in all conscience, but the interactions across these levels of equilibrium are far more difficult to understand, powerful and perpetual though they be.

Clearly, symbolically directed behavior channels our intervention in the ecological equilibrium; and experience of what does happen when we interact with the natural world feeds back into our vocabularies and concepts in such a way as to alter and correct, refine and redefine the symbols we use to guide our further behavior. Practical applications of natural science stand as evidence of how powerful this process can be; but in the deeper past, theological and magical ideas guided human actions just as efficaciously as science has done in recent times. Moreover, rules about when to plant or how to guard against disaster were corrected and adjusted in the light of results, just as we do today.

But, as I said before, symbols also define human roles and groups—friend and foe, relative, stranger, trading partner, fellow believer, fellow soldier, fellow citizen, and the like. The rise and fall of groups within a civilization and among civilizations is the substance of human history. Much is self-contained; i.e., created by the flow of messages in which our conscious lives are immersed. Yet there are constraints and pressures on our equilibrium of symbols that come from without. Some messages work, whereas others fail to achieve satisfactory results for those who act on them. These constraints arise from nature—animate and inanimate—and also from human nature; that is, from the ecological and physiological levels of our lives. No one, I think, is able to handle these hierarchical equilibria interactions very comfortably. Yet there are interesting convergences between these speculations about society and those which brain physiologists have advanced about how the cells of our brains produce consciousness and memory. Perhaps some day thinkers will be able to put each level together with its fellows in a far more satisfying way than I am able to do. If so, a firmer theory of social process, and with it of world history, will become attainable.

Short of that, and we are indeed far from any such synthesis, it nevertheless seems obvious to me that macrohistorians, in seeking to anatomize social process more accurately, are pressing forward on one of the more active fronts of intellectual invention in our time. This is the first or, at most, the second generation that could seriously attempt world history, if only because it is within this century that scholarly description and analysis of the various nonwestern societies began to achieve globality. It is, likewise, the first generation in which sufficient detachment from naive ethnocentrism has become possible, largely because the self-confidence of western peoples was so shaken by World Wars I and II, and by the fearful prospect of World War III.

To find oneself in such a position is both exhilarating and oppressive. We may be in process of formulating views that will seem classical to generations yet unborn. We may simply be brushed aside by dogmatic simplifiers in search of a simple orthodoxy, enforceable through police power. Or we may merely become quaint as our ideas and formulations become completely outmoded through the further evolution of human knowledge and belief. Time alone will tell.

# Part Two

*The Need for*
*World History*

# Four

# A Defense of World
History

World history was once taken for granted as the only sensible basis for understanding the past. Christians could do no other than begin with creation and fit subsequent details into the framework of divine revelation. This ordering of the past survived into the seventeenth century as Bossuet and Walter Raleigh may remind us. But with the revival of antique letters, a different model for historical writing asserted itself that could not fit smoothly within the Christian epos. In effect, Thucydides and Tacitus challenged Augustine, presenting the history of states and their interaction as a self-contained whole. Guicciardini and Machiavelli wrote their histories accordingly, dismissing as irrelevant the world historical framework that had seemed essential to earlier believers.

First given as a Prothero Lecture, 1 July 1981, and reprinted, with minor editorial changes, from Royal Historical Society, *Transactions,* 5th ser., vol 32, 1982.

In the eighteenth century a secularized version of the Christian vision of universal history found expression, especially in France. Progress was substituted for Providence. To be sure there was much room for difference of opinion as to what constituted progress; but then there had been wide differences of opinion as to how to fit the facts of history into biblical revelation, too. The important thing was that the essential unity and linearity of the Providential, Christian view of human experience on earth remained intact. With the nineteenth century, however, reaction against French cultural and political primacy found expression in nationalistic national histories. The fact that governments kept records and began to make them accessible to scholars assisted this development; so did the expanding power of the national state over everyday life in the most active centers of European civilization. The vaunted scientific criticism of sources by nineteenth-century scholars therefore developed very largely inside governmental archives. As a result academic history as it became institutionalized, first in Germany and subsequently in other European countries, was well and truly captured by the record-manufacturing and record-keeping bureaucracies that sustain modern states.

Insofar as governments matter in human affairs, there was nothing wrong with such a marriage of convenience. Governments did matter more and more as the nineteenth century turned into the twentieth; and the national frame within which nearly all academic history had been cast therefore did not appear particularly constrictive or inadequate. On the contrary, keep-

ing up with the flood of documents any modern government generates became a task to daunt even the
most industrious historian. Those who tried had no
time to think, or, indeed, to notice that bureaucratic
output of ink-soiled paper does not and never has embraced all the parameters of human life with which historians might appropriately concern themselves.

Medievalists, at least, were always wiser inasmuch as
national states mattered less, if, indeed, fifteen hundred to five hundred years ago, anything plausibly to
be called a national state could be discerned at all. Local
communities on the one hand and "universal" institutions—Church and Empire—on the other, played such
prominent roles that they could never be dismissed
from the center of attention. Church-state polarities remain even in our secularized age, as recent events in
Poland and Iran illustrate. Other, less firmly institutionalized groupings also continue to affect public life
profoundly. Languages, for example, only occasionally
and quite imperfectly match up with political jurisdic-
tions, as any speaker of English ought to recognize.
The shading off from mother tongue to Koiné for use
when dealing with strangers, together with the facility
with which a specialized technical vocabulary can develop among experts and become unintelligible to outsiders, makes language a protean and yet uniquely
human medium of communication. Since shared meanings, disseminated through communications networks,
are what shape and govern collective human behavior,
historians ought always to take language groups seriously into consideration. Messages transmitted with-

in governmental bureaucracies are only a small part of the communications net that ought to constitute our concern.

Though shared languages and messages conveyed in words are the most important element in fixing behavior, they are not alone in binding human beings together into structured wholes. Civilizations and cultures also exist; and most civilizations embrace speakers of several different and mutually incomprehensible languages. Conquest of one people by another was the usual way linguistic pluralism arose in civilized societies. But, when communications were weak, linguistic diversification could occur by imperceptible evolution across time. This happened among the speakers of romance languages in Europe, for example, and among the Sanscrit speakers of India as well. But linguistic pluralism, whether evolutionary or resulting from conquest, need not disguise what we may call the stylistic coherence of a civilization. Such coherence arises from key commitments to organizing, dominating values, and to institutions that express such values. Consequently, religious texts and rituals are often more clearly indicative of civilizational identities than other facets of human behavior. But art styles, technology, and quite secular forms of association—caste, family, polity—are also important elements of civilization and have a role in maintaining its coherence. When they leave tangible traces, as art and technology do, their territorial and temporal distribution help historians to define boundaries between one civilization and another rather more sensitively than written texts ordinarily permit.

However complicated and massive they may be, civilizations are not self-sufficient entities, either. Important interactions run across civilizational boundaries, and always have. This is no more than one should expect. For whenever a person encounters something curious and new, and especially when the novelty also appears to be superior to what had been familiar before, the only intelligent response is to do something about it. One may try to appropriate the new thing and make it one's own by learning how to make and use it. Porcelain spread from China in this fashion; guns diffused around the world on the same basis; and so did sewing machines and motor cars and thousands of other such modern devices.

But if the novelty seems wicked or dangerous and repugnant to existing commitments within one's own society, what then? One can try to disregard the offending persons and things, and hope they will not come again; or seek to drive them away by force. But to exclude a genuinely attractive novelty usually calls for strengthening local skills and institutions. As a minimum, repudiation requires more strenuous policing of ports or of the people's minds. As a maximum, radical revolution masquerades in reactionary guise.

As a matter of fact, beleaguered societies seldom dare or care to borrow what threatens them directly. Japan did so after 1868; Russia did so on three successive occasions under Ivan the Terrible, Peter the Great, and Stalin. But successful revolutions from above are rare, whereas reactionary reforms of the sort Khomeini seeks are far more popular, and, coming from below, are often capable of generating long-last-

ing, far-reaching change. Ironically, efforts to escape
the toils of alien corruption often end by incorporat-
ing important elements from abroad. Ayatollah Khomeini's movement, for example, took hold in Iran
thanks to tape recordings of his sermons which escaped
the shah's police. And since taking power, the Islamic
fundamentalists have used television and radio to fasten
their hold on the people's mind with a virtuosity that
might make New York's Madison Avenue advertisers
envious. Despite their intentions, Iran will never be the
seat of traditional Shi'a piety again after such an experience. And from the other side, it is also the case that
the most earnest and heartfelt efforts to imitate some
foreign model can never entirely succeed in eliminating
telltale traces of older, traditional local patterns of
human interaction. The modern history of Japan, Russia, and Turkey should suffice to tell us that.

Thus, whether people accept or reject what is alien
and new to them, encounter with bearers of another
culture or civilization is sure to change local ways of
life. This was and remains, in my opinion, the main
drive wheel of historical change. Human communities,
left to themselves, are very prone to settle towards a
fixed routine. What prevents routinization is either
disturbing encounters with strangers or else an ecological crisis, when interaction with the natural environment runs up against some unforeseen limit. Since
encounters with strangers are far more frequent than
ecological crises, strangers' alien ways are what mainly
compel and induce men to alter their behavior, thereby
creating historical change and maintaining its momentum across the centuries.

Societies situated in places where such encounters were unusually frequent pioneered civilization; and civilizations are distinguished from simpler forms of society by the fact that stimulating and disturbing encounters with strangers remained numerous and important throughout civilized history. Indeed, civilizations eventually made their bearers such strangers one to another that in our own age an autocatalytic process of social change within the body social seems to have set in. By now, for example, special research and development teams dedicated to changing the way we do things have about a century of permanent, bureaucratically institutionalized revolution behind them.

You may object that encounters with strangers only became important in recent centuries, beginning perhaps with the world-shaking overseas expansion of Europe. The cultural encounter between Europeans and the rest of the world's peoples is indeed the central axis of modern history, even if we ordinarily study it from a rather lopsided perspective. But similarly critical encounters are as old as civilization itself, and indeed older. At the beginning of civilized history, for example, when Sumerian cities became the seats of skills hitherto unknown among men, neighbors near and far took note and felt both attracted and threatened by the power of Sumerian metallurgy and Sumerian theology. Doubtless other aspects of Sumerian civilization also affected the peoples round about. *Gilgamesh,* the oldest surviving epic, for example, describes how Enkidu, the wild man of the steppes, was quite literally seduced to the ways of civilization by a harlot's charms. But if we discount the historicity of that text, we are left with firm and clear evidence for metallurgy and theology, but not for much else.

The prestige of Sumerian metallurgy is attested by the fact that Indo-European-speaking barbarians of the Eurasian steppe started to make stone battle axes in shapes resembling Sumerian bronze prototypes, and then proceeded to carry their new weapons across much of Europe. These same barbarians accepted the Sumerian pantheon and made it their own, as later literary records from India, Greece, Rome, and the Celtic and Germanic peoples make obvious. For Sumer's Enlil, god of storm, has his analogues in Indra, Zeus, Jupiter, Thor, and the rest. Clearly, in the 3rd millennium B.C., when Sumerian theology was new, a system of belief that explained natural events as acts of will emanating from a politically ordered cluster of divine personalities, was a dazzlingly persuasive way to understand the world and (not incidentally) to control it by appropriate rites of propitiation and supplication. The advantages of socketed axes, whether made out of metal or of stone, were no less apparent, as the design of axes we use today still attests. Thus we see that some 5000 years ago Sumerian metallurgy and theology were too important, too powerful, too attractive to neglect. The resulting transformation of Indo-European tribesmen's ways of life was considerable; and the long range historical consequences remain operative to this day.

Indo-European borrowing and adaptation of Sumerian skills and ideas is no more than what one would expect on entirely *a priori* grounds. Cultural interaction ought to have accelerated and become more important as soon as significant differentiation of skills arose between richer and more powerful, i.e., more civilized, communities and their neighbors. When strangers exhibit skills that are definitely superior to one's own, the need to do something about it is difficult to deny. Cultural action and reaction therefore ought to have intensified from the time the first civilized centers appeared on the face of the earth. Our evidence suggests that this was, indeed, the case.

My contention, therefore, amounts to this: in recent as in ancient times, encounter with strangers was central to human history because that was what forwarded innovation, always and inevitably. Communities that refused to alter their ways in light of threats and promises arising from contacts with strangers were liable to extinction. Those who reacted intelligently by accepting new ideas and learning new skills—whether this meant reinforcing old ways and strengthening defenses, or, in emergency, abandoning the tried and true in favour of deliberate borrowing from abroad—were the people most likely to flourish and enlarge their hold upon the earth's resources.

If this is so, historians' fixity of attention on national and local affairs is misleading. The profession still needs, as in the Christian past, a vision of the ecumenical setting within which each separate national state and more local community lived and moved and had its being. Only consciousness of how the processes of cultural interaction were running in a given age can provide an adequate context for understanding national and local history. Centers of skill, after all, rise and fall. Other, new centers take their place.

The history of industrialization and the geographical

migration of industrial skills and organization in recent centuries is a relatively well known example of this phenomenon, since Great Britain's primacy was unusually pronounced in the first half of the nineteenth century, and the establishment of industrial skills on new ground in Europe, America, and Asia was rapid and dramatic, thanks to the intensified communications network created by the new industrial technology itself. Cities of northern Italy enjoyed an earlier, less pronounced and somewhat lengthier economic and cultural dominion over much of the European peninsula, between, say, A.D. 1100 and 1600. Still earlier, when communications were less well developed, dominating centers of power and wealth migrated within the Mediterranean lands in a familiar pattern: shifting from the Syrian coast to the Aegean, and from the Aegean to Italy with the successive rise of Greek city states and the Roman empire.

Moreover, these European metropolitan centers, with their accompanying cultural slopes and barbarous peripheries, arose in a broader Eurasian setting where other styles of civilization were doing much the same thing in other favorable environments. Europeans entered into contacts with these other civilizations sporadically but significantly from the very beginning. Minoan connections with Egypt and with Asia Minor are well known; ancient Greek art derived key stimulus from the statuary of Egypt; and, as Juvenal complained, the Syrian Orontes later flowed into the Tiber. About the time of the Christian era, caravan trade across Asia created a slender, direct link between Syria and northwest China. At nearly the same time, sea voyaging attained a new intensity and level of organization, connecting the South China coast with the shores of the Indian ocean, and India with Egypt and the Mediterranean. Short overland portages across Malaya, south India and Suez raised costs and restricted the volume of this trade, but did not inhibit important exchanges of ideas and techniques as well as of goods.

Proof of such exchanges are not far to seek. The contribution of mass-produced Greek statuary to Buddhist art, and its subsequent stylistic transmogrifications in course of transmission across Asia, are well known episodes of art history. Simultaneously, religious aspiration in which Hellenistic and Jewish, Hellenistic and Persian, Hellenistic and Indian ideas merged and mingled gave birth to three powerful missionary religions, namely, Christianity, Zoroastrianism, and Mahayana Buddhism. Reaction against Hellenism also hardened Judaism into an enduring, rabbinical form, and helped to generate Islam. Subsequent Eurasian history turned, in no small degree, on how civilized populations reacted to these rival faiths.

But this is no place to recapitulate the landmarks of world history. Suffice it to say that sensitive attention to human reactions to encounters with strangers provides a powerful key to that history. Moreover, such encounters altered systematically from time to time, whenever some new technology of transport created new paths of communication and contact. The cavalry revolution of the ninth century B.C., for example, gave an importance and centrality to the peoples of the steppe analogous to the importance and centrality conferred upon western Europe by the navigational achievements of the fifteenth century. Railways, airplanes, rockets and electromagnetic communications belong in this same category of world-transforming breakthroughs. Each in its time altered the shape of older communications nets and thereby transformed patterns of cultural interaction and growth. Here lies the core and kernel of world history. Here are the structures within which local affairs can and ought to be understood.

All this may sound painfully *a priori*. Many historians, indeed, refuse to interest themselves in world history because they feel it involves so much vagueness and generality that testable statements about the past simply slip away. Such a view is quite wrong. World history depends on sources in exactly the same way as national or any other scale of history depends on sources; and the effort to corroborate or refute a particular hypothesis is the same, whether the hypothesis in question pertains to the entire world, to a civilization, to a nation or to some little village in the Pyrenees.

What constitutes adequate evidence is always problematical. One-to-one correspondence between a historian's statements and what "really" happened is unattainable; and if it were attainable would be undesirable, since it would simply preserve the buzzing, blooming confusion of everyday experience that impinges differently on every human being, hour by hour and minute by minute. A total recording of an individual consciousness is impossible, as novelists' experiments of the early twentieth century surely suffice to prove. What is needed—always—is a suitable shorthand: a system of terms that classifies experience into meaningful, usable, and satisfying patterns. Only so can we understand the world around us. Only by leaving things out, and lumping varying individual instances together into categories and classes of things, can we hope to navigate successfully amidst the infinitely various actual encounters humans have with one another and with the world around.

Language does this for us. Its capacity to generalize and order experience is built into every word we use. This is what makes human beings so incredibly powerful compared to all other forms of life. To be sure, the question still remains, whether terms available for world history—civilization, communications net, metropolitan center, cultural slope and the rest—are adequate to organize the observable experience of humanity on a global scale. Certainly there is room for improvement; and across time one can expect that historians and other students of society will develop new terms and modify those in use today. Language and learning evolve like everything else; and no one supposes that we have reached the end of the process of conceptual evolution.

Well, you may say, until someone has perfected a science of society capable of making all the variety of human historical experience fully intelligible, world history remains treacherously vague and so should be eschewed. But all other kinds of history are liable to the same reproach. Who can say that terms we use for national histories are unambiguous and adequate to all the facts? The very notion of government or nation, of Parliament and Crown, of public opinion and GNP embrace innumerable anomalies and variations of behavior on the part of individuals and groups of individuals. Full precision and exactitude escape such terms. It is their virtue that they erase what is judged by their users to be trivial differences and minor perturbations from norms and average patterns of conduct. That is what gives these terms their real, inescapably blurred, but nonetheless very useful meanings.

Epistemological exactitude is unattainable. To insist on it is an excuse for not thinking. For only by using inexact words to organize confusion, lumping together a range of particulars that differ from one another in some degree or other, can the intellectual enterprise proceed at all. We inherit our words after all; and any single person can only modify transmitted vocabulary in very minor degree, lest he become unintelligible.

Moreover, it is worth insisting that just because a given term applies to a larger number of particulars than another term, it is not necessarily vaguer or less useful. The Kingdom of England is just as real as the city of London or the borough of Westminster, and for some purposes, the larger entity is both more definite and more important. In general, large-scale patterns are just as real as small-scale patterns. A tree is a tree. It is also several millions of cells and millions upon millions of molecules and atoms. But no one supposes that accurate description of a tree can only be attempted by describing all its cells, still less every molecule and atom. On the contrary, the tree is liable to disappear entirely if one tries to descend to such minutiae. Even when staying within the range of unassisted human eyesight we all recognize that even though every leaf is different, we do not become unacceptably vague by calling a tree a tree. Similarly, in recognizing each tree as part of a forest and the forest as part of an ecosphere that extends right round the globe, we change scale without necessarily losing precision of meaning.

The plain fact is that radically different patterns co-exist, each at its own appropriate scale. Different words are needed to describe these different patterns. That is all. Precision and truthfulness do not necessarily increase as the scale becomes smaller. Large-scale truths and patternings can be just as precise as small-scale observations and truths. To discern patterns at each scale, an appropriate distance between observer and observed is requisite. Appropriate instruments to assist the naked eye are often necessary in our encounter with the natural world. For history, instruments analogous to the microscope and satellite scanner are not usually available: we simply have our eyes and the traces men happen to have left behind them on the face of the earth. We have the sources, in short. What is variable is the conceptual sensitivity and frame of reference that we can bring to the interpretation of those sources. Our questions turn attention hither and thither, depending on what hypotheses we seek to test. Consequently, the history we derive from our interrogation of the sources will differ radically with the questions we ask, since we will be using similar or identical sources to answer different questions and confirm or contradict different hypothetical patternings of the past.

Perhaps a parable will make my point clearer. Once upon a time, when working on my PhD thesis, I found myself at loose ends in New York City on a 4th of July afternoon. The library was shut for the holiday, so I went for a stroll in Morningside Heights. Below me ran the Henry Hudson Parkway, crowded with cars. When I glanced down at it, to my amazement I observed that the stop-and-go traffic on the Parkway constituted a longitudinal wave, with nodes and anti-nodes spaced at regular intervals, moving along the Parkway at a pace considerably faster than any single vehicle could make its way along the crowded roadway. Ever since, when caught in stop-and-go traffic I console myself with the thought that my car is no more than a particle in another longitudinal wave.

Few if any of the drivers whose behavior created and sustained the longitudinal wave on the Henry Hudson Parkway were aware of that dimension of their condition. Yet the wave pattern was most certainly there— clear and unambiguous. To recognize it required an observer, located at an appropriate distance, who possessed, ready-made, the notion of longitudinal wave with which to generalize the infinite detail that assailed my eyes as particular cars formed ever-changing geometrical relations to one another. Observer, scale of observation and concept all entered into the act of recognition. Without the fortuitous coming together of all three, the wave would have existed without being known.

Ever since, this chance experience has symbolized for me what large-scale historical study may hope to achieve. With appropriate concepts and sensitivity, a questioning historian can stumble on significant patterns in the past of which men of the age were often quite unaware, which yet are real and testable and important because they may endure for centuries and

millennia and affect civilizations and continents, so as
to constitute, like the ecosystem itself, an ever changing framework within which human history as a whole
runs its course. For who can doubt that human societies
are also constrained in ways analogous to the constraints upon the drivers in that traffic jam that pro-
duced such a strikingly regular, unexpectedly elegant
geometric result? To be sure, historical patterns are not
as simple nor as apparent as that long-vanished longitudinal wave. But that merely makes the study of history
more complicated as well as more interesting than the
science of wave mechanics.

All in all, there is nothing very mysterious to historians
in looking for patterns in the past and finding them.
We do it all the time. Nevertheless, before I close let
me try to bring the argument down to earth and establish the professional respectability of world history
more firmly by citing an example of large-scale historical hypothesis-making and testing from my own recent experience.

Some time ago, I wrote a book on modern Greece in
which I argued that perturbations in an age-old symbiosis between hill and plain provided the principal
driving force behind guerrilla outbreaks in Greece and
in the western Balkans generally. Sheep herders living
in mountain villages depended for part of their annual
food supply on exchanging surplus protein for calorie-
rich carbohydrates available from crop farmers in the
plains. Each party benefited from this exchange when it
functioned smoothly. But the shepherds were acutely
vulnerable to any interruption of the trade. Farmers,

after all, could subsist indefinitely with a lowered protein intake; but without imported calories, the shepherds faced imminent starvation. Within a few months of the breakdown of peaceable exchange, therefore, the hill villagers had no alternative to taking arms in hand, seeking to seize by force what they needed to keep alive. Hence the Balkan record of sporadic guerrilla outbreaks, dating back at least to the eighteenth century, triggered and enhanced by varying ideological commitments in recurrent times of crisis.

A few months afterwards I was trying to adjust my mind to a new understanding of what had happened in Sung China after about A.D. 1000 when the rise of an exchange economy brought ordinary peasants into the marketplace and allowed a great expansion of wealth. Wholesale exchange of Chinese grain for animals and animal products available to the nomads of the eastern steppe was a simple geographical extension of the commercial mutation of the eleventh century within China proper. Texts from the mid-fifteenth century showed that by that time at least Mongol tribesmen depended on grain from China for part of their annual intake of food. They had assimilated their condition to that of Greek shepherds, in short; and the pattern of protein-carbohydrate exchange was as advantageous in the Far East as in the Balkans—and as precarious.

Abruptly, a simple, grand hypothesis burst upon my mind's eye. What if this symbiosis of steppe and sown dated back to a time shortly before the age of Genghis Khan? If so, it would go far to explain the Mongol conquest of China, just as a similar symbiosis explains the sporadic outbreak of guerrilla warfare in the Balkans. For such a trade pattern would, when new, have allowed a larger number of herdsmen to survive on the steppes by increasing their food supply beyond anything they could produce locally and for themselves. And such an enlarged nomad population would have very strong motives for invading agricultural lands whenever interruption of grain deliveries occurred. Starvation was their only alternative, as it was for the shepherd communities of the Greek mountains who could not live the year around on the local produce of their herds, even when supplemented by cultivation of whatever arable ground lay within village boundaries.

Here was a grand hypothesis that cried aloud for testing. The obvious place to look was in Chinese gazetteers and other treatises. But I do not read Chinese. Fortunately, a former student who had worked with me at the University of Chicago, who is now a professor at the University of Hawaii, became interested and spent six months or so searching likely places in Chinese historical sources. Alas, he found no early signs of any grain export to the steppe and I now conclude that the Mongols learned to eat grain and supplement the products of their herds only after they had conquered China, not before. So my bright idea collapsed. The hypothesis had to be abandoned for the simple reason that no attestation in the sources could be found.

Some may feel that to depend on someone else to search the sources to prove or disprove an idea is unsatisfactory. For world history such cooperation is an obvious necessity, since no one, no matter how gifted, can ever master all the languages and other recondite skills that archeology and sister disciplines have now at their command. One simply must depend on others' results. Yet almost the same dependence on others holds for research in national and more local history. Ideas worth testing are a collegial, professional affair. Each historian depends on others—always. In crossing linguistic boundaries, such dependence becomes greater and more completely obvious. But to argue that no idea should be entertained that cannot be tested by oneself expresses an unrealistically solipsistic and indeed selfish attitude towards professional collaboration and mutual aid. Personally, I have no sense of disadvantage in relying on Professor T. Y. Tao to refute my hypothesis; on the contrary I feel immensely grateful to him that he paid me the compliment of thinking the idea was worth so much of his time and skill.

The pursuit of world history, therefore, conforms to the canons of our profession as far as I can see, and does so just as rigorously as history on any other scale. What is different is the conceptual frame and the geographic and temporal scope of the patterns one seeks to discern. In other respects, the method is identical; the validation the same; and the truthfulness of result neither greater nor less than what is attainable on other scales of history.

Is world history worth pursuing under such circumstances? Surely the answer is 'yes'. As the twentieth century draws towards its close, we live globally in a more intimate and pervasive sense than ever before, thanks to the acceleration and intensification of communication that has occurred in recent centuries. Consequently, the circumstances of our age demand a global account of how things got to be the way they are. Only so can the world in which we live make sense. To construct the best possible portrait of the whole human adventure on earth therefore constitutes a great and solemn duty historians should try to fulfill.

Men are and always have been myth makers, seizing upon the significant by leaving out the trivial, so as to make the world intelligible. If professional historians balk and refuse the role of global myth maker, whether from inertia or some mistaken scruple about supposed vagueness, others will surely move in to fill the void. For human minds imperiously demand historical experience to have shape and meaning—at least in retrospect—just because events as actually experienced in the present are so tumultuous, surprising, and unintelligible. They simply have to be given shape afterwards, or else are banished from human consciousness. After all, we have quite enough background noise to distract us, without worrying about the jumble that assailed our predecessors, unless, that is, their encounter with the world can be made intelligible by competent and conscientious historians.

Historians have in fact always performed this function for their fellows, and have habitually done so in universal terms. No more than a century ago, for example, patriotic English and American historians assumed that world history and their respective national histories were essentially the same. They believed that all humanity would in time learn the arts of self government as perfected under Queen Victoria or, as the case might be, by the Founding Fathers of the American Republic. History, in short, was the history of liberty, and turned upon how men had learned to restrain tyr-

anny and reconcile peace and order with individual
freedom. Ancient, medieval, and modern history were
shaped to this view. Attention focused on the critical
transactions in the history of liberty and left out everything else. Times and peoples who had played no part
in the constitutional development of Britain and America were banished from the pages of the meaningful
past on the specious ground that although tyrannous
rulers came and went, nothing really changed in Africa, Asia, and other benighted parts of the earth. Such
regions joined the march of history only when Europeans arrived, bringing Christianity, free trade, and a
just colonial administration to set such peoples' feet on
the path toward civilization and eventual participation
in the benefits of liberty under law.

This caricature of the human adventure on earth still
governs the way history is usually studied in the United
States and Great Britain. To be sure, no one now sub-
scribes to such a narrowly ethnocentric vision of the
past. Perhaps it is for this reason, indeed, that teachers
have banished serious consideration of world history
from our schools, no longer believing what our great
grandfathers took for granted, but having no better
view to put in its place. While the historical profession
continued to distribute teaching attention in rough
conformity to the discredited liberal view of the meaning of the past, active research turned away in embar-
rassment from constitutional history, and concentrated
on a long series of minute, technical questions instead.
Of course, microscopic analysis has opened up interesting and important new perspectives on the past. But it
is no substitute for a vision of the whole any more than

analysis of the cell structure of trees can supplant the ecological study of forests. Both scales of understanding have their place. Both are needed for any really vigorous study, whether of trees or of the human past. For half a century or more, English-speaking historians have emphasized micro at the expense of macro history. It is time to redress the balance, lest the profession sink toward triviality and preoccupation with merely antiquarian detail.

Human minds yearn to understand things in the largest possible terms. The universality of this urge is attested by the universality of foundation myths, explaining how the world got to be the way it is. Few such myths were historical in the sense of recognizing changes after an initial act of creation had occurred. Only three ancient peoples achieved an appreciation of the mutability of human things that deserves to be called historical, to wit, the Jews, the Greeks, and the Chinese. Europeans are the heirs of the Jews and Greeks, and as such have long been historically minded. Moreover, as I remarked at the beginning of this lecture, until very recently European historical-mindedness sustained itself within a frame of universal meanings—providential, progressive, or liberal as the case might be.

The human need for such overall understanding did not disappear with World War I, when the liberal, Anglo-American ethnocentric vision of the meaning of history met its (belated) Waterloo. To be sure, professional historians failed to respond to that catastrophe, and did not seek seriously to repair and refurbish a view of the whole human adventure on earth. Anthropologists were much bolder between the wars, and it is from them that I borrowed most of my conceptual baggage. Such lags in adaptation within an intellectual set of ideas and preoccupations becomes firmly institutionalized, as the study of history was and is in our universities.

But, as I argued earlier in this paper, a community that fails to adapt to new experiences and unfamiliar encounters with outsiders is unlikely to flourish, and risks extinction. Professional historians are in such a position today. Who besides ourselves really cares for the details that fill our learned journals and monographs? Why should we expect to be paid for doing things no one cares much about? Why should students listen to us? Why should anyone? Only when detailed researches are connected with a hypothesis that does purport to make the world make sense can the historical profession be said to earn its keep by performing its role as maker and tester of myths worthily. In the nineteenth century, when national states were still in the making, our predecessors rendered that service to eager generations of Germans, Americans, yes, and Englishmen (or should I say Britons?) too, by creating national histories for their respective constituencies and locating them firmly within a universal frame that in every case derived from a simple secularization of the Christian epos.

It is high time for historians to reflect anew about how the world's history can be adequately conceived. If we do so in the next few decades, the profession will again have something important to say to the public, and our place among the learned will be renewed and

assured once more. If we refuse to look for larger patterns and reject the possibility or desirability of world
history, nothing much may happen. A slow withdrawal
of resources, as interest in our private, professional preoccupations wanes among the general public, is likely,
but might come slowly, almost imperceptibly.

All the same it seems clear, at least to me, that unless historians seek actively and energetically to construct a credible portrait of the human past on a global
scale, we will have failed to perform our professional
function adequately. We cannot afford to make the
world in which our fellow citizens live historically unintelligible. We cannot afford to obstruct the effort to
achieve a credible view of the human past by insisting
on excessive detail that merely obscures the global
structure and patterns within which human communities exist and always have existed. I therefore commend world history to your serious attention. It is not a
luxury but a necessity, both for our profession and for
our time.

# Five

## *Beyond Western Civilization: Rebuilding the Survey*

I come before this meeting not because I have anything new to say, but because what I have to say seems to me sufficiently important to bear repetition. In the *A.H.A. Newsletter* for March, 1976, I wrote a little essay entitled "History for Citizens," and what I wish to say here and now is no more than a reaffirmation and repetition of what I said there.

I am not really apologetic, since if I am right in the diagnosis of our professional condition that I made in that essay, our discipline is in danger of slipping away from the privileged position it has hitherto occupied in high school and college curricula. Indeed, if we cannot turn the tide, we and any successors who undertake study of peoples beyond the national borders may find

Delivered at the annual meeting of the American Historical Association, 1976, as part of a panel on teaching, and reprinted from *The History Teacher* X, 1977.

ourselves relegated to the margins, where a few oddly curious students will seek us out in the way we have been accustomed to seeing classicists sought out, by a tiny handful of unusually motivated individuals whose fewness keeps classics departments small. I must say that it takes more imagination than I possess to think of a time when the study of history would become as marginal as the study of Greek and Latin language and literature is in our institutions of higher learning today; but if we persist in offering undergraduate students a rich diet consisting largely of the fine fruit of our private researches and expect them to be interested in demographic reconstitution of old parishes, the metal trades of Nuremberg, or the latest nuances of interwar diplomacy as revealed by newly declassified foreign office files, then I think the historical profession in America will deserve to be relegated to the fringes of higher education, and those of us not yet on tenure had better abandon history and seek another career at once and without further ado.

The only thing that can rescue us from such a fate is to find something worth teaching to undergraduates en masse: something all educated persons should know; something every active citizen ought to be familiar with in order to conduct his life well and perform his public duties effectively.

National history was invented for this purpose and still continues to fulfill a useful function, protected often by state laws requiring high schools to teach United States history to all students. National history may sometimes be badly taught, sanitized so that anything offensive to any pressure group that can get to textbook publishers is carefully excised from the record. But there is little chance that the patriotic tradition that sustains compulsory courses in U.S. history will not continue to give history instruction a privileged place at the high school level. This is a strategic advantage, no doubt, as against other disciplines seeking entry into high school classrooms. But there is a risk as well. For if such courses are poorly taught, students in college, given a chance to choose courses freely, will stay away from history like the plague. This may, in fact, have happened in the 1960s. In the course of that decade college and university historians surrendered their privileged position as teachers of compulsory courses—and did so without a fight, for the most part. College students became free to avoid history—and did so in such numbers as to exacerbate the job crisis our junior colleagues face so cruelly. Nothing I have heard in the 1970s convinces me that this rebound effect is not still working against us, and powerfully, too.

The reasons our profession did not defend the privileged position for history in the curriculum we had inherited from an older generation's empire building was that most historians had lost interest in teaching an introductory survey course. Young scholars wanted to escape the stigma of indentured labor; professors wanted to teach something of their own. No one was very happy with the intellectual presuppositions behind the existing surveys, whether in United States history or Western Civilization. Above all, no one thought it his or her responsibility to think of something better to do instead.

That is the central failure of our profession in the last two decades. So busy with research and exploration of new forms of history, often on a more and more minute scale because refined techniques required narrowing of vision, historians in this country seem to have been unable or unwilling to devote much effort to thinking about how to improve existing survey courses for freshmen and sophomores, or invent new ones that might be capable both of speaking to the concerns of the rising generation and of commanding the enthusiasm of those asked to teach such courses.

Doubtless any such sweeping indictment overlooks worthy and admirable efforts scores or perhaps hundreds of isolated historians have made to invent a new basic course. But in a more important sense I think the indictment still will stand: for whatever private personal efforts there may have been, the new courses that resulted have not been able to achieve a normative standing so as to spread from campus to campus with suitable modification and variation to fit local needs. Yet that is what happened in the 1930s and 1940s, when Western Civilization was rising to prominence so triumphantly. Whatever efforts individuals may have made to respond constructively to the need for finding a valid general introductory course in history for undergraduates at large, the profession as a whole as well as deans, chairmen, and other academic authorities, did not recognize the validity of whatever may have been proffered. New courses died a-borning, or became one of a thousand flowers allowed to bloom in departmental course listings by indulgent chairmen and generous budgetary officers.

The profession, in short, did not recognize any obligation to find something of general importance to teach all students. Each historian's course was presumed to be as good as everyone else's. It seemed professionally insulting to deny the right of any holder of the Ph.D. union card to do their thing with any and every undergraduate who might drift in, attracted by the course title, the professor's reputation—whether for easy grades or scholarly distinction—and the way the class hour fitted the schedule of other classes.

So, we cut our own throats, acting on the implausible proposition that intensive exposure to the chapters of a Ph.D. dissertation, slightly glossed, was as good for students as any mere survey course. After all, instructors teaching their own dissertations could really know what they were talking about, and thus avoid all errors, hateful oversimplification, and unfounded generalization. Besides, by keeping teaching close to research, the scholar could reasonably expect to publish early and often, and thus advance his or her career, if need be, at the expense of the students. For surely it is self-evident that according to these principles, history became intellectually precise only by becoming trivial as far as the interests of ordinary undergraduates and future citizens were concerned.

I need not say that this microscopic view of what makes histories true seems to me a sad misunderstanding of what historians do in making the past intelligible. Rather, I claim that each scale of history has an appropriate conceptualization and amount of detail, just as each scale of map has an appropriate projection and amount of detail. And just as a map is not a replica of reality, but a schematic representation of selected features from the relevant landscapes, so a history, too, is not a replica of what really happened, but a verbal construct that makes intelligible what is otherwise a confused jumble of potentially infinite and thoroughly unmanageable information.

If this is what historians do, the level of accuracy attainable does not increase automatically as the scope in space and time diminishes. Adequate schematizations of tiny themes may be easier, especially when a model of how someone else handled data for a similar topic or time span is available and commands respect. (I remember how, when I was a graduate student, one of my professors always invited his students to take on another railroad, and write a thesis by simply transferring the professor's own vocabulary worked out in his own history of the Illinois Central Railroad to the data provided by another railroad's files. Yet he attracted few students to a task which called for minimal inventiveness and maximal industry. Ever since, this has stood in my mind's eye as an example of how not to do Ph.D. theses and how not to study history. But this is beside the point.)

What matters, it seems to me, is the adequacy of the organizing concepts, the key terms, the point of view brought to bear upon the subject matter of study. An adequate organizing principle can make a world history or a national history just as accurate and far more exciting than any Ph.D. thesis is likely to be. In the not-so-far-distant past, our forerunners did invent a great idea about the whole human past. They saw all history as moving toward the realization of human freedom, and

were able to direct attention in the light of this idea to
the critical episodes and periods, places and transactions that constituted the principal turning points in
that story. The late-lamented survey of western civilization was a curricular embodiment of that idea,
though the clear focus of Lord Acton's generation had
already been lost when the Western Civilization course
was invented, and other matter soon so overlaid the
original organizing structure that most who taught
and, I suppose, nearly everyone who took such courses,
remained unaware of the principle that had once governed the distribution of attention—what was put in
and what left out. And just because the original idea
had been forgotten, these courses ceased to have any
obvious justification, and were surrendered gladly by
almost all who had been teaching them when some
bold spirits challenged the right of historians to inflict
what had become a hodge-podge of oddly assorted facts
and opinions on innocent undergraduates.

What our profession ought to have done, surely, was
to think again and see whether there was not some
other way of organizing a course of general significance
for undergraduates, or whether the old idea, if refur-
bished and suitably criticized, might not again sustain
a meaningful course. So far as I know, we did nothing
of the sort, and have not even responded to the fairly
widespread student withdrawal from our classrooms by
doing much more than complain. Indeed, the profession seems far readier to try to set up an effective lobby
with state legislatures so as to assure legal protection
against encroaching "social studies" than we are to undertake the intellectual work of trying for a new course

which we could defend with conviction against any and all critics as a suitable and proper building-block in every young person's education.

If it is really true that we cannot agree upon some kind of general course, then it seems to me that historians are saying to the rest of academia that we have nothing to teach young people that they ought to know. To say, "Take any of a score of different courses, differing in content, point of view, emotional color and intellectual rigor," is simply not an answer that anyone outside the profession will take seriously—nor should they. If all we have to say to the young is what individual scholars and idiosyncratic teachers care to put into their courses, then history as a key element in everyone's education does not exist. No one can take all such courses; if each is as good as the others, and all but one or two are dispensable, then in logic all are dispensable! And it takes no more than an average level of critical acumen to arrive at that conclusion.

As I stand here today, I must confess that it seems to me self-evident, as it did fifteen years ago when I started work on *The Rise of the West,* that the only frame suitable for introducing students to the world in which they live is world history. It seems to me obvious that beyond the national frame we must have a genuinely global history to offer the young—or else fall short of the imperatives of our time, when affairs of Africa, China, Vietnam, or any other part of the globe may acquire critical importance for public life and demand an informed judgment of ordinary citizens.

I have no doubt, for instance, that the ill-fated adventures of the American government on the continent

of Asia since 1950 have been facilitated by the massive
ignorance of those countries that prevailed in the upper
echelons of government and society, not to mention the
innocence of the American rank-and-file for whom Asia
was as unknown as Darkest Africa had been for the early Victorians.

Yet what have historians done to move into this gap?
Mighty little, I regret to say; and those efforts that have
been made were the work of isolated, idiosyncratic individuals, who have not given birth to contagious
course structures that could sweep the country as Western Civ once did. No such sweep will occur unless and
until the historians of this land agree that a world history course is possible, desirable, and important. I
think that most historians today do not believe any of
these things and have not thought seriously at all of
what it is we ought to be teaching students who do not
intend to become professional historians, and who in all
probability will never take another history course or
even read a book of history once they escape from our
hands. Can anyone really doubt that such persons need
to know something about the way the heirs of the great
cultures of the past differ from us and among themselves? And how can historians teach students something about these things except on a world scale?

As I say, these propositions seem self-evident to me,
and I am surprised that so few have done anything to
try to meet the need. I find the apathy truly amazing;
suicidal; absurd. Maybe I should be less surprised than
I am at the folly of the historical profession; after all,
historians are human and the past bears ample testimony to humanity's capacity for folly. But when pro-

fessional self-interest is so clearly at stake, when intellectual imperatives point so clearly in the same direction, and when the difficulty and delights of the effort are so challenging, it does seem surprising to me that so very few historians of this country have tried to teach world history, argued for it, interested themselves in it, or done anything at all to move outside their chosen specialisms.

Well, my Jeremiad is now at an end. I could offer suggestions for models of world history in addition to that which I have myself worked out; but this is not what I think most important. What is needed is a multiplex effort on many different campuses to do something intellectually serious and practically effective to invent a new basic course that will be meaningful in itself and useful to all students, capable of commanding the loyalty of those who teach it, and important enough that historians can argue once more for a greater share of student time.

Without such a course to teach to students of any and every specialism, the place of history in our colleges and universities is going to continue to shrink, almost for sure. What have you done to make that dismal future less likely? That is the question each of us ought to ask, those here and those far more numerous outside of this room. Doctors, perhaps, can afford to become narrow specialists, for at least they can still sometimes cure a patient through their specialized skills; yet even they have been much criticized for the loss of contact with ordinary human beings that their concern with narrow specialism involves. How much more vulnerable is our profession to that reproach?

Why should the American public be conned into paying our salaries if we have nothing to say to them? Why indeed? Specialists talking only to specialists have a place in the profession as we all know and recognize; but the ultimate justification for such behavior is that specialists' ideas and data filter down to others, who can use them for testing and correcting broadly interpretative history useful to the general public. A pyramid without a base is a *lusus naturae;* that, it seems to me, is what the historical profession has tried to become. Small wonder that we see the edifice tumbling down.

# Part Three

*Masters of the*
*Historical Craft*

# Six

✳

# *Lord Acton*

John Emerich Edward Dalberg-Acton (1834–1902) steeped himself in paradox. In an age of rising nationalisms, he was an Englishman by choice; but by birth, education, and friendships he remained a cosmopolitan Catholic aristocrat who was as much at home in Germany, Italy, or France as in England. In Acton's youth, Pope Pius IX went to great lengths to draw the line between Catholic truth and Liberal error, and nearly all liberals reciprocated by regarding the Roman Catholic church as the principal obstacle in the path of progress. Yet, to the scandal of fellow Catholics and the surprise of fellow liberals, Acton opted emphatically and in public for both. Then in his later years, he attained a great reputation as a historian, mainly on the

Reprinted from *Lord Acton, Essays in the Liberal Interpretation of History,* edited by William H. McNeill, © 1967 by the University of Chicago.

strength of a book he never wrote. Nevertheless, Acton's inclusion in this series, not to mention a continued flow of books about him, successive reprints of his essays, and frequent quotation of his aphorisms, all attest to his power of exciting interest (and usually admiration) across the better part of a century—a time sufficient to eclipse the names of many historians far more prolific than he.

Acton's fame rested and continues to rest partly on his social position and personal connections. On his father's side he descended from an English Catholic *émigré* who had enjoyed a spectacular career in the service of the King of Naples, in which city Acton was born. On his mother's side, he descended from one of the noblest families of southern Germany, the Dalbergs. When Acton was three years old his father died. Three years later his mother remarried, taking as her second husband an English Whig aristocrat who was only nineteen years older than her son. Acton's stepfather, the second Earl of Granville, inherited a political position in England that allowed him, as a matter of course, to arrange for Acton to occupy a seat in Parliament as soon as his education was finished. Granville himself was a member of almost every Liberal Cabinet formed between 1840 and 1886, and climaxed his career by twice holding the post of Foreign Secretary, in 1870–74 and in 1880–85.

Despite these family connections, no less than three Cambridge colleges refused to admit the young Acton—presumably because the dons of Cambridge feared that his Catholicism might precipitate scandalous conversions to Rome like those with which John

Henry, later Cardinal, Newman had recently disturbed the peace of Oxford's quadrangles. As a result, at the age of fifteen, Acton went to Munich to live and study with the Catholic priest and historian, Professor Ignaz Döllinger.

Acton lived in Döllinger's house for seven years. Even when the university was not in session, he continued to enjoy Father Döllnger's company on trips to various cities of Europe, where the two combed archives and secondhand bookstores for rare or forgotten materials pertaining to almost every aspect of modern history. Döllinger and his precocious pupil varied their scholarly activity with social calls upon the great and near great of the age, whose doors opened automatically to a brilliant young man with Acton's family connections. The basis for Acton's magnificent private library (60,000 volumes at his death) was laid during these vacation trips; his later fame for knowing everything and everyone of any importance in Europe was based upon this same experience.

From his studies with Döllinger, Acton acquired one preeminent conviction: to wit, that the Church, like other institutions, had undergone and would doubtless continue to undergo important changes across the centuries. German historical scholarship had made it clear that the Church had not always and everywhere remained the same; but this view of ecclesiastical reality was unfamiliar among English Catholics. Upon the completion of his formal education the young Acton therefore resolved to begin a journalistic career in order to communicate this message, together with other fruits of his continental sophistication and learning, to his insular fellow churchmen. He did so as coeditor of, and contributor to, first the *Rambler* and then the *Home and Foreign Review*. By 1864, however, the tone of these journals had aroused the public ire of the Archbishop of Westminster, the Roman Catholic Primate of England. Acton thereupon decided to retire from the fray, and two years later also abandoned his parliamentary career.

A surprisingly large proportion of Acton's published work dates back to these early years, when weighty essays, polemical reviews, and learned trifles like the study of Charles II's illegitimate son poured easily from his pen. Many of Acton's mature traits were demonstrated in these early essays—in particular, his ability to stand aloof even in dealing with matters like ultramontanism with which he was himself deeply and personally involved. He looked from two perspectives, but both seemed in focus, for the historian's dispassionate and Olympian vision, measuring men and events against the rich tapestry of the past, helped rather than hindered the polemicist's sharp thrust. Acton profoundly believed that, when properly understood, Catholic truth and human liberty did not conflict but were mutually dependent. Without an autonomous and international Church to counterbalance political power, he felt that constitutional liberties could never become genuinely secure. To guard against abuse, rulers had always to be checked and limited, and how better than by a divinely established suprapolitical corporation?

But after his collision with the Archbishop, this happy constellation of circumstances no longer sustained Acton's labors. His effort to mobilize accurate, scientific historical scholarship in the cause of liberal Catholicism having been rejected by his ecclesiastical superiors, Acton fell back upon aimless and desultory journalistic activity for a few years, but he put his main effort into behind-the-scenes negotiations, aimed at galvanizing the liberal forces within the Roman Catholic church into more effective action. Then, after 1870, when the viewpoints Acton had championed were resoundingly repudiated at the Vatican Council, he gave up journalism almost entirely.

Instead, he set himself the task of writing a great book that might deliver his message to a later age more ready to receive it. These, then, were the years when his magnum opus, *The History of Liberty,* was projected but not written. He read voraciously, took endless notes, hastened like a bird dog after every newly opened archive or freshly published work of historical scholarship, and fell, inevitably, farther and farther behind the task of mastering all the available information which might be relevant to his projected history. In 1877 he did sketch the main lines his book might have taken in two lectures on the history of freedom; and in private conversations he often ignited the imaginations of his hearers and amazed them with his erudition as he spoke of how the history of mankind could be understood as a tortuous yet persistent advance toward liberty.

Nevertheless, Acton's total failure to accomplish what he and his friends expected of him is the central fact of his life. His collected writings constitute mere slivers and fragments, occasional pieces and classroom lectures, which were thrown off casually and incidentally in the course of his titanic labor of self-preparation for the great work which he never even started.

Such a catastrophe is not inexplicable. In the first place, Acton's conception of the proper method of historical research made the writing of any large-scale history, dealing with many subjects across long periods of time, an utter impossibility. His extraordinary powers of memory and indefatigable reading habits perhaps allowed him at first to deceive himself about the practicability of realizing his ideal of accuracy in the light of *all* the sources; but by the 1880s such self-deception was no longer possible. Nevertheless, he could not, or at least did not, abandon his naive notion of how historical truth should be sought.

Let him speak for himself. In the concluding paragraphs of his *Lectures on the French Revolution,* he says:

> Where do we now stand, and what is the elevation that enables us to look down on men who, the other day, were high authorities? We are at the end, or near the end, of the supply of Memoirs; few are known to exist in manuscript. Apart from Spain, we are advanced in respect of diplomatic and international correspondence; and there is abundant private correspondence. . . . But we are only a little way in the movement for the production of the very acts of the government of revolutionary France.
>
> . . . One collection is coming out on the Elections for Paris, another on the Paris Electors. . . . Then there is a series of the acts of the Commune, of the several governing committees, of the Jac-

obins, of the war department, and seven volumes
on the Vendée alone.

In a few years all these publications will be
completed and *all will be known that ever can be
known*. [My italics!] Perhaps someone will then
compose a history as far beyond the latest we possess as Sorel, Aulard, Rambaud, Flammermont
are in advance of Taine and Sybel. . . . In that
golden age our historians will be sincere, and our
history certain. The worst will be known, and
then sentence need not be deferred. . . . Men-
dacity depended on concealment of evidence.
When that is at an end, fable departs with it, and
the margin of legitimate divergence is narrowed. [1]

Thus Truth, the whole Truth, is just around the corner, awaiting the publication of a few more sources.
Unaccountably, Acton seems to assume, even at the
very end of his life, that there is a definite and forseea-
ble limit to the number of sources that can be found
relevant to the study of such a complex reality as the
French Revolution, and he dismisses the historian's role
as architect, organizer, and interpreter of facts as mere
"fable." Yet, at the same time, the "sincere" historian,
knowing the truth, will have to judge the crimes and
moral failings of the men whose acts he describes; and,
knowing all, he must not shrink from pronouncing his
magistral, final, and eternal sentence. Acton, in fact,
reserves for the historian roles which Christian doctrine

1. *Lectures on the French Revolution* (London: Macmillan & Co.,
1925), pp. 372–73.

assigned to God himself: omniscience and final judgment. No wonder, then, that he concluded with a tacit confession of the vanity of his own ideal:

> We might wait long if we watched for the man who knows the whole truth and has the courage to speak it, who is careful of other interests besides his own, and labours to satisfy opponents, who can be liberal towards those who have erred, who have sinned, who have failed, and deal evenly with friend and foe—assuming that it would be possible for an honest historian to have a friend.[2]

Yet this explanation of Acton's failure is insufficient. Many solid and learned tomes were written by his contemporaries and successors who shared nearly the same view of historical method. If universal history was impossible, topical histories were not; and Acton had notes for a dozen or more such works, any one of which, if executed, would have found a valued place in the European historiographical tradition. Moreover, even if the task he set himself exceeded human powers, Acton might have started to write his great *History of Liberty* and ended his life with the first volumes behind and some untold number ahead—a fate which has befallen many historians before and since.

Because he did neither of these things, something more than mere methodological folly is needed to explain his inability to write the book he projected. Indeed, it seems to me that behind his frantic effort to

2. *Ibid.*

master all the sources we can discern a pervasive and paralyzing conflict between his moral and his intellectual judgments.

Morally, Acton was deeply committed all through his life to the enhancement of liberty for individuals and for small groups. He found the tyranny of the majority no less than the tyranny of kings and of prelates utterly repugnant. As a result, all the great men of history who had to smash their way through obstacles and overcome vested interests became evildoers. Virtue rested only with the defeated, who, Acton recognized, usually wished nothing more than to do to their conquerors what their conquerors had done to them. Nevertheless, facts were facts, and crimes uncommitted from want of opportunity were less heinous than those which were committed. Acton's strikingly ahistorical preoccupation with the historian's role as a "hanging judge," redressing the injustices of the past by measuring the deeds of rulers and mighty men against the universal yardstick of justice, was a tangible expression of his belief in an absolute morality and in the liberty which, he thought, that morality required.

But intellectually, Acton could not really persuade himself that the actual course of history fitted into the sort of liberal mold his moral principles demanded. Mankind's record, far from being a history of liberty, seemed rather to be a long history of the denial of liberty by any group strong enough to impose its will. In his early years, for example, Acton hailed the American Revolution and the Constitution which emerged in 1789 as the wisest and most perfect expression of liberal principles yet manifest on earth; but the upshot of

the American Civil War destroyed the federal principle
as he understood it, opening a way for tyrannical democratic majorities to override all opposition just as in
revolutionary and postrevolutionary France. If this were
the upshot of the wisest statesmanship the world had
yet seen, what hope could there be for Acton's brand of
liberty? Indeed, he must often have doubted whether
the British Constitution itself was the apex of political
wisdom and a practicable model for all mankind.
Knowing the history of Europe as intimately as he did,
British liberty seemed more like an insular oddity
which had been able to come into existence and survive
because the salt water of the English Channel reduced
the exigencies of war and lessened the need for standing
armies.

Acton saw quite clearly whence would come the
main challenge to liberty as domesticated in late Vic-
torian Britain.

> That which arose in Northern Europe about the
> time of our revolution settlement [that is, 1689]
> was a new form of practical absolutism. The-
> ological monarchy had done its time, and was
> now followed by military monarchy. Church and
> State had oppressed mankind together; hence-
> forth the State oppressed for its own sake. And
> this was the genuine idea that came in with the
> Renaissance, according to which the State alone
> governs, and all other things obey. Reformation
> had pushed religion to the front: but after two
> centuries the original theory, that government
> must be undivided and uncontrolled, began to
> prevail. It is a new type, not to be confounded
> with that of Henry VIII, Philip II or Lewis XIV,

and better adapted to a more rational and economic age. Government so understood is the intellectual guide of the nation, the promoter of
wealth, the teacher of knowledge, the guardian of
morality, the mainspring of the ascending movement of man. That is the tremendous power, sup-
ported by millions of bayonets, which grew up in
the days of which I have been speaking at Pe-
tersburg, and was developed, by much abler
minds, chiefly at Berlin; and it is the greatest
danger that remains to be encountered by the An-
glo-Saxon race.[3]

In such an encounter, could liberty, defined as respect
for individual rights and for minority privilege, hope to
prevail?

Acton, I think, was far from sure that history did
not, in fact, march with the big battalions and with the
absolute, concentrated power which, according to his
most famous aphorism, corrupts absolutely. But he
never had to meet his problem squarely because there
was always another document to consult before the
great *History of Liberty* could begin. Indeed, he may—
half consciously—have become a virtuoso of bibli-
ographical erudition in order to avoid having to confront the dilemma between power and virtue that his
innermost values—his vision of truth and of morality—presented to him.

Essentially the same problem haunts anyone today
who inherits western individualistic values and reflects
upon our advancing capacity to control and manipulate

3. *Lectures on Modern History* (London: Macmillan & Co., 1906),
p. 289.

one another. It is therefore possible in reading Lord
Acton's pages—amid much that seems ponderous,
dull, or outmoded—suddenly to come across a brief
passage or pithy saying in which one's own half-formu-
lated thoughts or feelings seem to attain a sharper definition or wider ranging expression than before. This
capacity for occasional scintillation, surely, constitutes
the basis of Acton's claim to rank among the great historians of Europe.

There was, however, another aspect of Acton's experience that probably had as much to do with paralyzing
his literary activity as any mere intellectual dilemma.
For Acton had an unusual emotional life. The early
death of his father and his mother's remarriage led to a
polite and relaxed but pervasive lack of sympathy between stepfather and stepson. This prepared the young
aristocrat to transfer a store of filial feeling to Father
Döllinger, the Munich professor who took him into his
house. And on the other side, a man of Döllinger's
bourgeois origin must have been deeply flattered by
Acton's ardor for learning and delight in his modest
company. Then, in Acton's middle age, after thirty
years of close association, climaxing in the period of the
Vatican Council (1869–70) when he and Döllinger had
stood together in trying to prevent the declaration of
papal infallibility, he went out of his way to pick a
quarrel with his friend and mentor. Wishes of the family long prevented the publication of Acton's correspondence with Döllinger,[4] but odd notes that Acton left

4. The first of four projected volumes of this correspondence
recently appeared. See Victor Conzemius, ed., *Ignaz von Döllinger
Briefwecksel mit Lord Acton, 1850–1869* (Munich: C. N. Beck Ver-
lagsbuchhandlung, 1963).

behind amid his enormous collection of papers make it
clear that this break was, for him, fraught with the
greatest emotion. Acton's reaction, indeed, was altogether out of proportion to the ostensible issue between the two men, for the point of difference was
whether a historian should judge everyone, prince or
pauper, guilty of murder if he had ever ordered or con-
trived a murder![5]

In later years, to be sure, Acton recovered his balance and began once more to write a few articles. From
1886 he became a contributor to the newly established
*English Historical Review,* and on the occasion of Döllinger's death was even able to analyze learnedly and
dispassionately the historical work of the man he had
quarreled with and yet revered. This is perhaps the
most remarkable example of Acton's ability to disguise
his personal feelings when writing as a historian.

Acton's learning and liberalism led in 1895 to his
appointment as Regius Professor of History at Cambridge. This position required him to deliver a famous
inaugural lecture—the ripest and most explicit state-
ment he ever made of his views of historical scholarship. He also prepared two series of public lectures,
one on modern history and the other on the French
Revolution, which were published after his death. But
his greatest impact upon the historical profession was
the result of an invitation issued by the Cambridge
University Press to plan and execute a modern history.
In Acton's hands this invitation turned into a vast col-

5. See Gertrude Himmelfarb, *Lord Acton: A Study in Conscience
and Politics* (Chicago: University of Chicago Press, 1952), pp.
147ff.

laborative effort, *The Cambridge Modern History*. Paradigmatically he died (1902) when the first volume was in press, and before he had himself written a projected introductory chapter.

Acton's influence, nevertheless, was far greater than might be expected. More than any other single man, he transplanted German thoroughness and historical method across the Channel. As a result, in the English universities writing history from anything but primary sources became unprofessional after Acton's time, as it had been in German academic circles from Ranke's days. In addition, so far as I can discover, Lord Acton was the first Englishman to view British, American, and Continental European history as a common whole, and to imprint upon this synthesis what Herbert Butterfield has aptly termed the Whig interpretation of history, that is, the notion that all mankind has been toiling onward and upward through time toward the pinnacle of English (and/or American) constitutional liberty. Acton presented this view in his public lectures on modern history and—at least implicitly—in his plan for *The Cambridge Modern History*. Thereby he set the mold within which the English-speaking world has tended to view modern times ever since.

The longevity of such a view is not really to be wondered at. Cross-fertilization of nineteenth-century German academic standards of historical research with the native English Whig view (which before Acton's time had been applied mainly within the parochial frame of British constitutional development) obviously created an interpretation of modern history which was both persuasive—"scientific"—and enormously flattering to the self-esteem of the entire English-speaking world. Moreover, the prestige first of Britain and more recently of the United States in international affairs assured that other peoples and men of deeply alien culture would learn their history from schoolbooks shaped into this mold as much by Acton as by any other single man.

Yet, with a final paradox, such a smugly certain, simple view of the past was precisely what Acton himself had never unambiguously enunciated or really been able to believe. His university lectures and his editorial planning lent themselves to this interpretation; his own essays never went so far, and his great masterpiece testified, by the fact that it remained unwritten, to Acton's inability to subscribe to the lessons which his students and admirers so readily drew from history.

World War I and the multiple disillusionments of the interwar years did much to discredit smug confidence in the progress of liberty and justice. Instead, the idea that history moves in cycles and that the heyday of liberalism was perhaps drawing ineluctably toward an end gained plausibility. Oswald Spengler in Germany proclaimed this view with relish; Arnold J. Toynbee in England concurred, but with reluctance. Yet these and similarly systematic schemata never won more than marginal and grudging acceptance among professional historians. Too many details did not fit. The result, therefore, of the dethronement of Whiggish history in the twentieth century has been to introduce a general confusion and intellectual uncertainty among historians. Contemporary historians lack the homogeneity of outlook that seems (at least in retrospect) to characterize those who wrote in Queen Victoria's day, for we are aware as our predecessors scarcely were of the historical reality and complexity of the non-Western world, and are committed viscerally if not always intellectually to the virtues of democratic government and liberal institutions, but remain at least as unsure as Acton ever was of whether history is a record of the advance of human freedom, of human power, of both freedom and power, or of power at the expense of freedom.

And because, like Acton himself, we have begun to doubt the adequacy of the Whiggish history inherited from Acton's age, his enigmatic, paradoxical, subtle, and erudite reputation has serenely survived. During his lifetime Acton became accustomed to survival amid the ruins of his own ambition; since his death his reputation appears to be equally invulnerable to the collapse of the view of modern history erected by his disciples and admirers. His greatness is perhaps sufficiently authenticated by these facts.

# Seven

## *Basic Assumptions of Toynbee's* A Study of History

There are at least three points of view from which the worth of a book of history may be assessed. One may ask whether the book is accurate; that is, whether it deals fairly and skillfully with the data upon which it is based. Secondly, one may turn the historian's characteristic tools back upon himself and ask: How did this book come to be written? What is its relation to the individual life of the author, and more particularly, what is its relation to the age in which he lived? And, thirdly, one may ask what basic ideas, assumptions, or intellectual methods may underlie the text, governing its scope and proportion, shaping its emphasis, and giving a sort of artistic or intellectual unity to the whole.

When, however, we attempt to focus upon a book so

Reprinted from Edward Gargan, ed., *The Intent of Toynbee's* A Study of History, (Chicago: Loyola University Press, 1961).

vast and various as Toynbee's *A Study of History* from any of these viewpoints, difficulties at once arise. His basic ideas seem to have shifted radically during the thirty-odd years he spent producing the ten volumes, so that many discrepancies between the earliest and latest volumes may be found. Moreover, our times are too much with us to make it possible to see his book clearly in relation to the currents of thought and feeling that still run among us. We cannot say which of the many contradictory strands will predominate or seem most significant to later generations. Finally, the scope of his inquiries is so wide, and his erudition so various, that the job of checking up on his accuracy must be resigned to experts in one or another of the fields of history with which he deals. Yet this is in some degree unjust, for errors of fact or judgment, which may seem monstrous to the narrow expert, need not necessarily invalidate the book as a whole. If we listen only to indignant specialists, the real greatness of the *Study* (which must surely lie in the effort to reduce all the multifariousness of human history to a comprehensible order) may quite escape us.

Indeed, on this point I venture the opinion, absurd though it may seem, that even if all but a few fragments of Toynbee's text should prove vulnerable to attack on the ground of factual inaccuracy, still the book will stand in the public eye, and also I believe in the judgment of posterity, as a notable monument of our century's intellectual history. Quite apart from the impression his ideas have made upon the lay public—and this in itself becomes an incident in the intellectual history of our times—Toynbee has presented the com-

munity of academic and professional historians with an
important challenge. It may or may not be taken up
seriously by future generations; and the long-term influence of his book will in part depend upon the reaction we and our successors make to the challenge he has
set before us.

The nature of Toynbee's challenge is twofold. First,
he has boldly overridden the conventional boundaries
between specialisms in the field of history. Taking all
the knowable human past as his province, he has found
rhythms and patterns which any less panoramic view
could scarcely have detected. I am, for myself, profoundly convinced that there are insights attainable by
taking large views of the past which cannot be had from
close inspection of the separated segments of history. I
once had an experience in New York City which for me
has come to stand as a symbol of the advantage which
may accrue to a man taking such an intellectual position. Once on a hot summer's evening when I was
walking on Morningside Heights looking down upon
the Hudson, the traffic on the Parkway beneath caught
my attention. It was heavy, and to my surprise I saw
that the cars were grouped along that ribbon of concrete in the alternating nodes and antinodes of a longitudinal wave, precisely like the diagram I remembered
from my physics textbook illustrating the propagation
of a sound wave. Moreover, the waves of traffic moved
along the Parkway at a rate considerably faster than the
progress of any car and were regular in length as well as
in their speed. Here was a truth about stop-and-go
driving on a crowded road which I had never known
before, even though I had more than once been a parti-

cle in such a jam. Only the long perspective of Morningside Heights permitted me to apprehend this aspect
of the phenomenon. Observers closer to the roadside
might see individual cars going by; might calculate
their speed or tabulate their makes, study the varieties
of hubcaps or measure the pollution of the air from the
exhausts; but from the very proximity of their vantage
points our imaginary observers could have understood
the wave-character of the traffic only through exact and
painstaking statistical analysis of a sort usually impossible in historical study from lack of sufficient data. Yet a
Toynbee-like vision of universal history, I believe,
opens the possibility of short-circuiting statistical
methods, as my glance from Morningside Heights
could do. New insights may arise with breadth of view;
fallible and never completely provable perhaps, yet
enormously stimulating to exact and careful study
which may find new questions to ask of familiar data in
the light of general ideas generated by men like
Toynbee. No multiplication of specialisms or narrowing down of fields of history in the interest of more
perfect accuracy can by itself hope to achieve such an
enrichment of our understanding of man's past. Interaction between large views, bold hypotheses, fallible
intuitions, and exact, detailed scholarship is what we
need. If we concentrate upon the latter alone, by drawing ever closer to the facts and seeing details ever more
completely, we may blind ourselves to other aspects of
reality. We may, in the terms of my parable, see only
the hubcaps and radiator grilles in the parade of traffic
and miss the waves entirely.

This, then, is the first great challenge which

Toynbee's *A Study of History* has put before us. It is a real challenge; for most academic historians, because they have made accuracy their major concern, have shrunk from universal history. After all, no man, not even a man as gifted as Toynbee, can hope to have more than a superficial acquaintance with all the fields of history; and until Toynbee came along, the English-speaking world had, for at least two generations, left universal history to brilliant amateurs like H. G. Wells, or, in this country, to the writers of under-graduate textbooks, whose efforts were directed not so much to new synthesis as to the cataloging of more or less well-assorted information culled from the work of specialists.

The second great challenge Toynbee has put before us is similar in that it constitutes a breakthrough of the traditional limits of our discipline, not horizontally, so to speak, but vertically. What I mean is this: Toynbee has felt himself free to connect his studies of history with ultimate philosophical and theological questions. His study of the human past has confronted him with such questions as: What is the destiny of mankind? What laws are human societies subject to? What part does God play in human affairs? Perhaps because we wished to be scientific, and were temperamentally cau-tious, professional historians have tended to skirt these major riddles of the human condition; but Toynbee has boldly rushed in where we have feared to tread and come up with his own individual answers. Quite apart from the question whether they are good answers or not, answers are there in his book; and I believe that much of his popularity arises from the explicitness with which he has confronted these ultimate questions which haunt, and have always haunted, the minds of reflective men.

We all know the enrichment which came to the traditions of political history when men began to delve into economic aspects of the past; and Toynbee, it seems to me, offers a similar enrichment by challenging us to bring our historical truths into relation with sociological, philosophical, and theological theories and beliefs.

Yet in attempting so grandiose a synthesis, accuracy of fact and accuracy of detailed interpretation inevitably suffer. Omniscience is beyond mankind, and in proportion as one ideal of history is emphasized another must be crowded into the shadows. This is, no doubt, the case with Toynbee, who, in undertaking to say something about everything, has laid himself open to expert criticism over and over again. Yet criticism directed merely toward correctness will miss the heart of his book, disguise its importance, and do little to explain (or to destroy) its significance for our age in general and for professional historians in particular.

Let me leave the matter of Toynbee's accuracy at that. However mistaken or wrong-headed he may be on particular points, the *Study* still stands before us, grand and imposing.

Perhaps we can hope to come nearer to an understanding of his significance by taking up the second critical standpoint, asking ourselves: How did this book come to be written? What is its relation to Toynbee's and our own time?

Two preliminary observations are perhaps worth

making in this connection. First, the scope and content of *A Study of History* is dependent on the work done by archeologists, much of it within the present century. If the goodly company of the archeologists had not discovered and studied Sumerian, Babylonian, Assyrian, Minoan, Mycenaean, Hittite, Indus, Shang, and Mayan civilizations, Toynbee could not have conceived history as he did. In this most elementary sense, his book is a product of our age. Secondly, the great popular reception his ideas have met in this country—a reception far warmer than they have had in England, or in any other country so far as I know—is undoubtedly connected with an easy inference to be made from his pattern of the development of civilizations. If the Western world is now becoming ripe for the emergence of a universal state, as his pages seem to suggest, the United States is clearly a contender for the role once played by Rome. Such a role flatters the national ego. If this is to become the American century, it is, to say the least, comforting to know the historical inevitability thereof in advance. In some influential quarters Toynbee's ideas were, I believe, so interpreted, and the publicity his books received depended in some measure upon this fact.

But these observations merely skirt the question of the relation between *A Study of History* and our times. Fortunately, Toynbee has himself given a reasonably clear account of how he first conceived the germ of the *Study*. In 1914, soon after the First World War broke upon an unsuspecting Europe, Toynbee, in the course of his academic duties as a young Oxford don, found the pages of Thucydides pregnant with new meanings, and applicable, with surprising precision, to the contemporary struggle in Europe. In Toynbee's own words:

> . . . suddenly my understanding was illuminated. The experience that we were having in our world now had been experienced by Thucydides in his world already. . . . Thucydides, it now appeared, had been over this ground before. He and his generation had been ahead of me and mine in the stage of historical experience we had respectively reached; . . . Whatever chronology might say, Thucydides' world and my world had now proved to be philosophically contemporary. And, if this were the true relation between the Graeco-Roman and the Western civilizations, might not the relation between all the civilizations known to us turn out to be the same?[1]

A sudden flash of insight, then, communicated from the pages of Thucydides in a time when the familiar landmarks of European civilization seemed about to collapse, raised a tantalizing question in Toynbee's mind; and as soon as the pressure of war duties in the British Foreign Office was removed, he set out to try to find an answer. If it were true that European historical development in the twentieth century A.D. was in some sense running parallel to the historical development of the Greek city-states of the fifth century B.C., was this mere accident, or part of a larger parallelism between

1. Arnold J. Toynbee, "My View of History," in *Civilization on Trial* (New York: Oxford University Press, 1948), pp. 7–8. See also Toynbee, *Study*, X, p. 94.

the whole life course of the two civilizations? And could similar parallels be discovered in the histories of other peoples? Was there, in short, a sort of plot or rhythm common to human civilizations?

As we all know, Toynbee's investigations gave affirmative answers to these questions. As early as 1921 he was able to jot down a draft outline of the work we know as *A Study of History,* and during the next eight years he worked out details and prepared notes to flesh out that preliminary outline.

During these germinative years, and down until 1933 when work on the first three volumes was completed, Toynbee remained strongly under the spell of the classical education he had received in school and at Oxford. This shows through quite clearly in the first three volumes, where he regularly used the history of the Greco-Roman world as the archetype and measuring rod against which to plot the careers of other civilizations. Indeed, the method he used to identify his separate civilizations was to search for analogs of the three leading phenomena which accompanied the decay of the ancient classical world—a universal state, a universal church, and barbarian invasions; and when some parallels to these phenomena were discovered, he was prepared to recognize the death of an older and the birth of a new civilization.

There is, here, a certain ambiguity in Toynbee's thought—or so it seems to me. He never gives a systematic, careful definition of what the term "civilization" means, but in later passages refers to it as a "state of the soul." Yet his criteria for recognizing separate civilizations are political, and as his book unfolds one discovers that the breakdowns of civilizations occur on the political plane also. I do not think Toynbee contradicts himself by such a procedure, for he could plausibly enough assert that the gross political manifestations which he used to discover the major outlines of the careers of civilizations were no more than outward and easily discovered manifestations of the state of the souls of the millions of men concerned with each civilization. Yet he has not spelled out what he means by his central concept of a civilization, and in his first three volumes he sometimes gives the impression that the political framework is at least for practical purposes identical with the civilization itself.

Such an emphasis upon politics is thoroughly in the tradition of classical thought; and there is still another sense in which his early inspiration derived from the ancients. From at least the time of Plato it had been a commonplace of Greek and Roman literature to hold that history moved in cycles. In its extreme form, as in the fourth of Virgil's *Eclogues,* this theory asserted that identical acts would recur time and again as the Great Year rolled round anew; in less fantastic form, men like Plato and Polybius held that constitutions underwent a regular cycle of change, rising toward an apex and then inevitably undergoing decay and eventual dissolution until the cycle began once more. Toynbee's view of the life pattern of civilizations, as advanced in his early volumes, was nothing but a translation of this classical commonplace onto a larger scene, substituting civilizations for the constitutions of city-states, and the globe, as known to contemporary Western historians, for the Mediterranean world of Plato and Polybius.

Yet however deeply Toynbee's mind in his early manhood was imbued with Greek and Roman literature, it remained true that, like Western civilization itself, his precocious childhood had been even more profoundly affected by exposure to an intense, evangelical Christianity, which gave him an abiding familiarity with the King James Bible. In the later 1930s when the progress of public events cast the long shadow of the Second World War upon the scene, and when personal problems also distressed him deeply, Toynbee's classicism began to wear thin. By degrees Toynbee the Hellenist gave way to Toynbee the man of religion, not quite Christian perhaps, since the creeds and formalism of organized Christianity repelled his mind. But still his new frame of mind may, I think, fairly be described as an enriched and sophisticated version of the Christianity of his childhood. One can see the beginning of this transformation in the middle group of his volumes, published on the eve of World War II, and the change in outlook became explicit and complete in the four concluding volumes published in 1954.

This gradual conversion was Toynbee's personal response to the challenge of personal sorrow and public disaster. The phrase from Aeschylus's *Agamemnon, "pathei mathos"* (learning through suffering), which had echoed in his mind even in his most Hellenized years, came to have an ever growing significance for his view of the history and destiny of mankind.[2] For through suffering, he came to believe, specially gifted men

2. Toynbee, *Study,* X, p. 235.

might attain a sensitivity, otherwise beyond their powers, to the divine reality behind mundane appearances; and, as teachers and prophets, could share their enhanced vision of the nature and purposes of God with their fellow men, whose minds had been readied for the reception of their message by the same suffering.

From this point of view, the cyclical rise and fall of civilizations came to have a new meaning. In his earlier, Hellenizing years, the recurrent breakdown and dissolution of civilizations had stood as a self-contained tragedy, attesting the limitations of human powers and the blindness of human passions. The consolation of history, as he then apprehended it, was a sort of Stoic heroism in the face of foreknown disaster. The three quotations which he prefixed to his first volumes: "Work...while it is day..."; "Nox ruit, Aenea..."; and "Thought shall be the harder, Heart the keener, Mood shall be the more, As our might lessens," accurately catch the tone of his mind, deeply affected as it then was by the war of 1914–1918.

But from his new standpoint of the later 1930s and after, this resigned pagan heroism began to seem mere blindness to the most basic reality of the world. Instead of being mere disaster, the long drawn-out human suffering involved in the dissolution of a civilization now appeared as the greatest of all challenges offered to men, creating for them the indispensable social matrix for reception of divine self-revelation. Thus the entire historic process changed its character in Toynbee's eyes. History was no longer simply cyclical; one civilization was no longer strictly equivalent to another. Instead, through the establishment of religions during the declining phases of a civilization's existence, a permanent addition to human knowledge of God was painfully attained. Universal history thus appeared as a gradual, stage-by-stage revelation of God to man. Religions replaced civilizations as the supremely valuable and significant forms of human association. God displaced man as the protagonist of history.

In this revised picture it is not difficult to recognize the lineaments of the traditional Judaic-Christian interpretation of history. Faith in progress, which Toynbee had rather scornfully rejected during his Hellenized years, was now restored, though not in its secularized eighteenth- and nineteenth-century form. To be sure the cycles of civilization remained; but they served, like the wheels of some great chariot, to carry humanity onward, ever onward toward some divinely appointed and unforeknowable but plainly desirable end.

The development of Toynbee's mind, in response to the public and private experiences of his mature lifetime, obviously involved discrepancies and changes of emphasis, if not outright contradictions, between the earliest and latest volumes of his *A Study of History*. These discrepancies may, perhaps, illustrate a changing temper of our times; I do not know. Certainly his growing religiosity is not unique; other sensitive spirits, too, have turned toward God as he has done; but whether he and they comprise only a minority in the intellectual community of our time, or whether they will appear in later times as pioneers of a new age remains to be seen. However that may be, Toynbee's volumes may be better understood and their discrepancies appreciated only if the reader sets them, as I have tried to do, against the background of the years in which they were written.

It remains, now, to take up our third vantage point and examine Toynbee's work in itself, asking what basic assumptions and intellectual methods underlie his book. It is here, I believe, that we can discover a measure of consistency and unity in his whole thought, despite the disparate conclusions which have at different stages of his life dominated his mind. For Toynbee the Hellenist and Toynbee the man of religion both used much the same methods of inquiry, and at least one common assumption underlies both the earlier and later versions of his vision of history.

Let me say something about Toynbee's methods of inquiry first, and turn to his assumptions at the end of this essay.

Toynbee likes to call himself an empiricist, and repeatedly describes his procedure in seeking illustrations for some general proposition about human history as an "empirical survey." Yet it seems to me that his use of this word is distinctly misleading. For his "empiricism" is an empiricism which already is keenly aware of what it is seeking; and in such a difficult and multifarious study as history, it is all too easy to find evidence to "prove" almost any proposition. The reason is simple. The potential data of history are limitless, and by selecting for attention only those bits and pieces that fit in with one's notions, a convincing "empirical" validation of the preconception with which one started out may often, if not always, be achieved. Yet this is the procedure by which Toynbee again and again seeks to prove or justify his generalizations. It follows, I think, that whatever value they may have—and in my opinion many of them have a great value—does not rest upon the empirical surveys of which he seems so fond.

Indeed, Toynbee's self-proclaimed empiricism seems to me largely a pose, adopted originally, perhaps, partly in an effort to distinguish his thought from Spengler's;[3] and one which has been largely abandoned in his later volumes. Rather, the heart of Toynbee's intellectual procedure has always been the sudden flash of insight such as that which, on his own account, launched him originally on *A Study of History*. The experience of suddenly seeing some new relationship or pattern emerging from a confusion of elements previously unrelated is one which I presume all thinking men experience from time to time; and such experiences often carry with them a considerable emotional force which almost compels assent even before the details and implications of the new insight have been tidily arranged and worked out. Such I conceive to have been the method by which Toynbee worked his way through history; and being endowed by nature with an unusually powerful memory and an even more powerful imagination, his flashes of original insight have been numerous and far ranging. Many of them are, at least for me, profoundly illuminating. Let me just mention two examples from European history where my information is adequate to make it possible for me to con-

3. Toynbee, "My View of History," pp. 9–11.

trol, in some measure, the data Toynbee worked upon. I find, for example, his concept of an abortive Far Western civilization on the Celtic fringe of Europe in the early Middle Ages, and his account of the competition between what he calls the "city-state cosmos" and the national state organization of late medieval and early modern Europe eminently enlightening. His analysis of the successive phases through which Greek and Roman society passed, and especially of the early phases of the growth of Greek civilization, seem to me masterful and entirely persuasive; and to go somewhat further afield, in his anatomy of the Ottoman Empire in particular and of nomad empires in general, he seems to me to be barking up the right tree, though his analysis may be a bit too schematic to fit each case exactly. It is passages such as these, where the free exercise of a synthetic imagination has succeeded in suggesting novel relationships or discerning new points of view, which, in my opinion, make Toynbee a truly great historian.

But I must also confess that there are other passages in his book where his imagination seems to run amok. In the interest of fitting his data into a pattern he sometimes seems to cut and slice reality in an arbitrary and even fantastic fashion. I will mention only one instance of this: his description of the Arab caliphate as the resumption of a Syriac universal state after a millennium of Hellenic intrusion does not convince me in the least. Yet once the equation is made, throughout the rest of the book it is baldly taken for granted, and the sense in which the caliphate was also heir to Greek and Roman culture is nowhere seriously taken into account.

Such contrasts as these point up the difficulties of

Toynbee's intellectual method. The sort of insights upon which the book is founded come in a flash or not at all, arising, in large part, from the hidden and unconscious levels of the mind.[4] Their nature is closer akin to the vision of the artist than to strictly rational or merely inductive mental processes. But rational and inductive processes contain their own controls, being bound by logic and sense perception; whereas the constructive imagination lacks such controls, and may go sadly astray by virtue of the very freedom which in lucky instances permits it to strike home to the truth.

My first point, then, about Toynbee's intellectual procedure is his reliance upon insight and imagination rather than upon arguments or induction. In this he is true to the Platonic intellectual tradition of which he is a latter-day representative; for Plato, too, and all good Platonists after him, have experienced and, having experienced, have valued above all else the flash of intellectual insight—the vision of the Idea—which Plato set as the apex of intellectual endeavor.

This suggests another important characteristic of Toynbee's procedure: for just as Plato in the *Republic* falls back upon a myth when he wishes to describe the Idea of the Good, so also Toynbee at critical points in his book resorts to myth and metaphor, and finds in these an otherwise unattainable path to the solution of problems he has set himself.

I need scarcely remind you of the freedom with which he resorts to these devices. Images such as the

4. See *Study,* VII, p. x, for an account of the subconscious prologue to Toynbee's first drafting of his *Study.*

elaborate metaphor of the climbers on the rock face or the pollarded willow of the first volume give a picturesque sharpness to his concepts; and, more than this, seem sometimes for their author to take on an independent life and reality of their own. Toynbee's mind tends to move freely among visual images, metaphors, and figures of speech, finding baldly abstract and severely verbal formulae a pallid substitute for fully embodied imagination.

One may, indeed, say that his habit of mind is poetic, and it would be a mistake not to recognize his book as a prose epic, whatever else it may be besides. If his literary style were more austere and polished, his book could, I think, stand comparison with Dante, or better, with Milton. Indeed, in Toynbee's own spirit one might make up a table of literary parallels: As Herodotus is to Homer, and as Thucydides is to Aeschylus, so Toynbee is to Milton. Like Milton, he combines classical humanism with evangelical religion; but Toynbee lacks the doctrinal certainty of his predecessor. In much the same way the two great Greek historians accepted the fundamental intellectual framework of their poetic forerunners, but could not accept the pantheon of Olympus.

Toynbee's use of myth as a guide and suggestion to argument occurs at critical turning points in his book rather than throughout. But in falling back on Goethe's *Faust* for hints as to the manner in which a civilization comes into being, in summoning Aeschylus's Prometheus to assist him in comprehending the processes of civilization's growth (III, 112 ff.), or in resorting to the language of Christian theology when discussing the relations of law and freedom in history, Toynbee is reproducing for his readers the processes of mind through which he himself passed in order to arrive at his conclusion.[5]

Toynbee has confessed that this procedure at first filled him with misgiving, flying, as it did, in the face of accepted, scientific, sober-minded, intellectual method. But whether by birth or training, he found peculiar stimulus in the world of poetry and myth, and decided to plunge ahead and follow the suggestions that came to him from these sources in plotting out the drama of human history. In later years, he found a theoretical justification for what he had done. "I have now lived to see," he writes, "the subconscious well-spring of Poetry and Prophecy restored to honour in the Western World by the genius of C. G. Jung; but, before Jung's star at last rose above my horizon, Plato's example . . . had given me courage to part company with an early-twentieth-century Western Zeitgeist whose . . . only realities were those that could be weighed and measured."[6]

As I understand Toynbee's mature conviction (and I am not sure that I do understand his rather oblique and fleeting references to this arcanum of his thought), mythology represents an attempt to express in figurative and narrative language an intuitive grasp of the deepest reality of the human condition: a reality which can tamely but only inadequately be expressed in sober, severely intellectual discourse. And since the intellect

5. Toynbee, "My View of History," p. 11.
6. Toynbee, *Study*, X, p. 228.

is only part of man, and not necessarily the most far-ranging or reliable part at that, he now feels that he was right in relying upon the inspiration of myths to guide his thoughts, for they represent free intuitions of the soul, whose universal value has been tested by their survival through many ages and countless retellings.

For my present purposes, however, there is no need to explore or to criticize Toynbee's *ex post facto* justification for his procedure. The important point is the procedure itself—a movement of mind and method of thought very deeply implanted in him, and as characteristic of his early Hellenized as of his more recent Christianized outlook.

I think he would agree that Plato is his intellectual master of masters; and this is true not only in his reliance upon flashes of insight, and in his use of metaphor and of myth to convey or suggest meanings which sober matter-of-fact language leaves lifeless, but also in the habit of mind which strives in the face of all the diversity of experience and of history to arrive at the interconnectedness of things—to see multiplicity and discrepancy reduced to unity and order, to see the whole in the parts, the One in the Many. This is, indeed, the most basic and fundamental quality of Toynbee's mind, a quality perhaps unusual in an historian, who is normally liable to be arrested and intrigued by the variety and multiplicity of things and to take the data of history more or less for what they are—infinitely various, changeable, shifting, and interesting.

The impulse to find a unity in history implies, of course, that there is such a unity to be discovered; and this seems to me to be the bedrock of Toynbee's entire intellectual enterprise. Here is the basic assumption of his *A Study of History:* that there is an intelligible unity behind all the diversity of human historical experience. Moreover, it is possible to characterize the unity Toynbee believes he has discovered; for alike in his earlier as in his later phases of thought, he has seen history as essentially a drama in which the human spirit is confronted with an Other, suffers frustration, and is provoked to respond by changing itself, thus growing, or, when the response falls short of success, suffering decay; but in either case making history. The nature of the Other which confronts the human spirit may vary: it may be physical nature, it may be other men, it may be God; and the later phases of his thought are distinguished from the earlier by the greater emphasis he now puts on the third of these alternatives. Yet in the fundamental picture of the historic process, and in the assumption that there is a Form or Idea (in the Platonic sense) to that process, he has remained entirely consistent, so far as I can see, from beginning to end.

I must confess that I am myself sufficiently close-wedded to the Zeitgeist of the twentieth century to be disturbed by some of Toynbee's mythological and theological language. Yet I find it possible to extract sound sense from his pages. History, I agree, is change, and change in human society is, I believe, provoked by challenges (of whatever sort) from outside the closed circle of custom and institutional precedent which binds the normal day-by-day life of men together. And the reality of rhythms and patterns in history I am not disposed to deny. No doubt such crude paraphrase

would, for Toynbee himself, lose all the barely ex-
pressible overtones and utterly distort the truth he has
sought to convey. Such imperfect communication is,
however, normal in intellectual discourse and should
surprise no one. My point is merely this: I find much
scintillating suggestion and stimulation to thought in
Toynbee's pages; he has opened vistas of history and
put questions before me as no other single author has
done. For this I am grateful, and insofar as he does the
like for others of the historical profession, we should all
be grateful. He has certainly not spared himself in pursuing a high goal. I hope that future historians may
find inspiration in his example, and will test, criticize,
correct, and not entirely forget to emulate his efforts. If
we do, the study of history cannot fail to be enriched,
and we will worthily uphold Clio's oft-disputed claim
to reign a queen among the sciences.

# Eight

✳

## *Carl Becker*

Forty-four years have passed since I came here to study history under Carl Becker; and returning to lecture, not to listen, is a little spooky. Memories, filtered and framed by subsequent experience, crowd round; and their vivacity is enhanced by the fact that I chose as my subject three historians who helped to shape my mind and whom I met here at Cornell in three different ways: Becker in the flesh, Toynbee through the first three volumes of *A Study in History;* and Braudel spectrally, through the writings of one of his mentors, Marc Bloch.

Is it an ill omen that Becker comes first? Turning my thoughts to him is perhaps quixotic in this place where his shade still walks and where living members of the faculty have edited his papers and studied his

This and the following two chapters were prepared for delivery as the Carl Becker lectures at Cornell University, Spring 1983.

thought professionally, whereas all I have to go on are some spavined recollections and a recent, repentant look at the corpus of his published work. There is further risk in the fact that by a selective reaction to what he had to say, I may merely succeed in cutting Becker down to my own size, misunderstanding him in my own way just as those who have already written about Carl Lotus Becker seem to me to have done.

But once committed to the quest, knights errant need must err I suppose, or at least risk error. So let me proceed, without fear and without research, to tilt at windmills of my own making. Becker as he really was remains, in any case, beyond reach. His own principles make that clear. What I can try to anatomize instead is his meaning for me; a tiny episode in intellectual history, but delicate and difficult enough inasmuch as it involves human interaction across a generation gap and within a now quite vanished climate of opinion framed by the two great wars of this century.

I have no recollection whatever of first meeting Carl Becker. Instead, his name calls two memories to mind, one probably dating from my first year here, 1939–40, and the second dating certainly from the fall of 1940 when I was his teaching assistant.

The first vision takes me back to an afternoon meeting of his seminar. Becker was at the head of the table, and I sat on his immediate left. Perhaps half a dozen other graduate students had gathered to hear what he had to tell us. The announced theme of his seminar that year was historiography; but we seldom met, for Becker was chronically ill and cancelled meetings more often than not. But on this particular afternoon he had made his way to campus with a heavily corrected typescript in hand, and from where I sat I could see how words had been changed, phrases moved back and forth, and whole passages stricken out and rewritten. He read from his text for an hour or more, every so often losing his place amidst the tangled corrections, or pausing to decipher scribbled emendations. I remember nothing about discussion afterwards. Presumably, it was desultory. For Becker's theme that afternoon was the concept of creation and cosmic recurrence as recorded in ancient Hindu and Buddhist texts. Such silly stories did not interest me, and Becker's summary of them remained remote from anything I knew or cared about. He was no expert in these matters, as he freely admitted; and I thought it showed. Altogether, a puzzling performance from a man reputed great.

Callow incomprehension thus prevailed in Mr. Becker's seminar that year—at least as far as I was concerned. Looking back now I much regret that he did not bother to explain what he was up to. Perhaps he assumed that we had read his book review/essay "What is Historiography?" published in the *American Historical Review* in the year before I came to Cornell. There Becker described how the history of histories, if conceived with more detachment than Harry Elmer Barnes had brought to the task, might become a "phase of intellectual history" by forgetting "entirely about the contributions of historians to present knowledge" and concentrating instead "upon their role in the cultural pattern of their own time." Such an approach, Becker had suggested, would reveal the "gradual expansion of the time and space frame of reference which in some fashion conditions the range and quality of human thought."[1] But I had not read that little essay. Others present showed no sign of having done so either; and I certainly lacked the perspicacity to see anything worthwhile in Becker's paraphrase and commentary on Indian myths. It is ironic now for me to realize how utterly I failed to appreciate his effort to transcend the limitation of the European-American world where all his previous work had centered. I was not then ready for such a venture; and the way Becker presented it left me cold.

His obvious difficulty in writing English sentences also surprised me, and may even have been vaguely disquieting. My habit was to write rapidly and correct hastily. The way the words fell onto the page was good enough for me as long as they seemed grammatical on rereading. Yet here was a man who surely wrote well and still couldn't get things right the first time! How odd! I wish I could say that Becker's example inspired me to more careful correction of my own prose; but that is not so. Several years later, in 1952 to be exact, I discovered belatedly that I could improve a manuscript I was readying for the press simply by combing out passive voice constructions. Since then more and more ways of writing badly have come to my attention, and my manuscripts begin to approach the crabbedness of those pages I could see from where I sat at Carl Becker's side in his seminar years ago. But, alas, it is easier to imitate Becker in messing up a manuscript than it is to attain his limpid felicity of phrase.

1. Carl L. Becker, "What Is Historiography?", in *American Historical Review*, 44 (1938), p. 25.

So much for my first image. The second is even less satisfactory, for in the autumn of 1940, as the Battle of Britain wound down and war visibly approached U.S. shores, Mr. Becker taught his last undergraduate class somewhere in Boardman Hall. I can see him still, a little, balding figure, seated behind a desk, head bent low over his notes, mumbling on and on in a barely audible monotone about the French Revolution and Napoleon. As his assistant, my job was to take daily attendance and each week to distribute a blurred mimeograph sheet, prepared who knows how many years before, that summarized what Becker was about to say in his next few lectures. Each sheet also listed quantities of additional reading, to which no one paid attention.

I found the ritual quite as wearisome as Becker seemed to. Of course, blotted ink and blurred letters did not prevent the weekly precis from remaining beautifully clear—too clear, perhaps, for human affairs are not nearly as tidy as was Becker's mind. But for students looking ahead to an exam, clarity and brevity were a great comfort. Simply memorizing the contents of a slender sheaf of fifteen mimeographed pages provided Becker's students with everything they needed to pass the course. Sitting quietly in class was a price to be paid, but students were biddable then as they are again today. For the really ambitious, there was Gershoy's textbook, which treated everything summarized in the weekly precis at much greater length. Indeed, rumor among Cornell graduate students held that Gershoy had used Becker's mimeographs—the very same I handed out—to write his book, having first checked to make sure that Becker no longer planned on turning his lectures into a book. Whether that is true I cannot say; nothing in Becker's published correspondence seems to support the idea. But that was how we accounted for the resemblance.

Why did he teach so badly? It seemed unpardonable then and it seems so still. Each tattered capsule I distributed to the class was insulated from anything he was thinking about at the time, being no more than a deposit from a then quite distant past, dredged up anew for uncomprehending and indifferent undergraduates; rightly indifferent, I must say, since Becker only expected them to regurgitate scraps from his mimeographed sheets on quizzes afterwards. For someone who held the life of the mind so dear and whose own internal dialogue was so intense, such an abdication seems altogether out of character.

I can only suppose that in a time long before I knew him, institutional constraints required professors to lecture, though Becker's intense shyness made that act terribly painful. Failure to communicate viva voce taught him to rely on written precis of what he was going to say; and once they took form—I presume in his early days at Cornell—duty and convention required him to continue the ritual of meeting classes, whether his lectures served any useful purpose or not. The suggested readings were there for anyone who might by some chance become really interested. What more was there to do?

Perhaps, indeed, the drive to write well that carried him to such heights was tied up with his equally conspicuous failure as a lecturer. Shyness, so inhibiting in public speech, often arises from overweening self-esteem—self-esteem that makes its victim feel unsure of being recognized or accepted by others at anything like his own valuation. As a student, Becker probably did suffer from overdoses both of insecurity and of self-esteem; and as a professor he made up for failure in the lecture hall by more intense effort in his study. So maybe he would never have disciplined himself to write so well if he had not been painfully inadequate in class: who knows?

Nevertheless, Becker's mien in the classroom, however deplorable, was not the only difficulty I faced in reacting positively to his teaching. The fact was that I had heard it all before—from Louis Gottschalk at the University of Chicago, whose version of modern European history was almost as faithful to Becker as Gershoy's textbook was. Nor in listening to Gottschalk was I encountering Becker's thought-world for the first time. That happened in 1932 when I took modern history in high school, and read Becker's then new-minted textbook from cover to cover.

Anyone seeking to assay Becker's influence in American life ought to begin with that textbook, whose blocky pages and bright green cover remain clearly etched in my memory. *The Heavenly City* and his other famous writings affected professional historians rather than the general public, whereas his textbook was so widely used that it must have gone far to shape my generation's vision of the European past—so far as we have one at all. Moreover, when European history faded out of high schools and become a college subject after World War II, Robert Palmer, another Carl Becker student, wrote the textbook that still reigns supreme in the field. Palmer, to be sure, was no mere carbon copy of Carl Becker, yet it is also true that he reaffirmed and elaborated an architectonic of modern European history that Becker raised initially by searching for a meaningful national past for the United States on *both* sides of the Atlantic. Thus it transpires that ever since 1931, first Becker and then one of his pupils did more than anyone else to introduce Americans to European history. It follows that whatever ideas the American public may have today about Europe's past derive more from Becker than from any other single mind.

Given human aptitude for misunderstanding written and spoken words, such a proposition is probably unverifiable; but were I a scientific historian I would deluge you with statistics of textbook sales since 1931 to back up the suggestion. However, my theme is not Becker as he really was, nor his historical importance, real as that may have been; I confine myself to his meaning for me. And in reflecting on that, I conclude that his high school textbook did indeed provide the principal basis for all I have subsequently thought and written about European history. My negativity in the presence of the great man in 1939–41 drew much of its force from the fact that I had by then already begun the process of modification and amendment to Becker's portrait of Europe's past to which my professional life has been devoted; and being conscious of points of divergence, I was blind to the fundamental continuity. I was the last and probably one of the more intractable of his pupils, quite unable and unwilling at the time to recognize my debt to him because it was against aspects of that heritage that I was in revolt.

Revolt began early, for I recall being shocked at how cavalierly Becker's textbook dismissed the Puritan revolution of the 17th century. The English civil wars got less than a page; the whole Puritan movement became a mere episode in the Age of Kings and Nobles, and marked no fundamental advance of liberty, nor of any other good thing, since Britain remained oligarchic and monarchical. My Scots Presbyterian acculturation in Canada had accorded even English Puritans at least presumptive title to the sainthood they aspired to. So I complained to the teacher about how Cromwell got too short a shrift in the textbook. His response was to invite me to repair the deficiency, so a week or two later I talked to the class about the English civil wars, drawing my information, as I recall, exclusively from a red–bound copy of G. M. Trevelyan's *England under the Stuarts* which my father provided from his library. My first lecture; my first revision. Reactionary of course, because I merely reaffirmed views that Becker had rejected when his youthful encounter with puritanical Methodism gave way during his college days to Enlightenment ideals.

During my first year at Cornell, a different kind of revisionism gathered momentum in my mind. Lectures by Philip Mosely and Marc Szeftel introduced me to the history of Russia, Poland, and the Balkans. These lands obviously marched to a different drummer from whatever it was that set the rhythms of historical development in the west. Neo-serfdom came to eastern Europe after serfdom had disappeared from the west; renaissance and reformation were far to seek; and, according to Mosely, the Russian revolution was not a belated and perfected version of the French revolution, as I had been prepared to believe, but had instead set up a heavy-handed police regime, whose xenophobia and wasteful use of human resources were more reminiscent of Ivan the Terrible and Peter the Great than of Marx or even of Robespierre. I can remember quizzing Mosely after class on this point, provoking a brief account of his personal encounters with police in rural Russia during the middle 1930s that was concrete and completely convincing.

Here, then, was a far more important discrepancy between expectation and credible testimony than Becker's brisk dismissal of Cromwell had ever been. The awkward fact was that the version of modern history enshrined in Becker's textbook and therefore in my head in 1939 had no room for countries that did not advance liberty or even contribute to industrialization, save laggardly with Five Year Plans of 1928, 1932, and 1937. Becker had viewed eastern Europe from outside, treating its states simply as military-diplomatic pieces in the age-old game of balance of power. But at Cornell a new perspective opened and with it a new problem of trying to understand how social evolution east and west could follow such different paths. All I have subsequently done in European history revolves around this question; but it was years later, and only after encountering Toynbee and Braudel—among others—that something like a coherent answer took form in my mind.

Mosely and Szeftel had no easy answers to my questions, but what they taught me about eastern Europe quite exploded the snug synthesis of modern European history I carried thither—a synthesis that I now realize had come largely from the way Becker had deftly juxtaposed quite discrepant older traditions in his textbook and in his teaching of my teachers. On rereading that textbook in preparation for this lecture, three different angles of vision upon the European past fairly leaped from its pages, though when I first read it I was completely unaware of any such thing, still less of the conceptual problem of reconciling one with another. Becker himself surely knew what he was up to, and never ceased to worry about how the diverse heritages of his own age could be combined in a way that would make modern civilization worth preserving, or even trying to preserve.

Such worries passed me by in 1932—and subsequently. Instead, I lapped up the textbook's information and rejoiced in the strikingly simple, tidy structure that Becker gave to modern times. First came the Age of Kings and Nobles, when state-building and balance of power prevailed. Then came the Age of Political Revolution, when the advance of liberty and democracy gave new meaning to old forms of political struggle. Finally in the Age of Industrial Revolution, science and machines changed the conditions of human life, provoking social conflict at home and imperialism abroad. The story came to a particularly confusing climax with World War I when Europe was "turned upside down in order to make the world safe for democracy." History as past politics, history as the progress of

liberty, and history as the record of changing relations
to the means of production thus were combined within
the covers of a single book by the simple device of as-
signing each predominance in a given chronological period. Foreshadowing of the age to come was part of the
scheme, for the democratic revolution "was accomplished in men's minds before they made it the work of
their hands," to quote the title of one of Becker's chapters; and, of course, the industrial revolution began
long before 1871 when Becker started its "Age."
Carryover from earlier ages was no less real. Balance of
power survived the birth of liberty in 1789, and balance of power *and* liberty both persisted into the industrial age. But the relationship between the old and the
newly dominant trends of European history remained
profoundly ambiguous. Apparently, that amibiguity
remained acute in Becker's mind from 1918, or before,
until the day he died. His biographers have already explored the fluctuation of his mood with respect to liberty, class war, and international balance of power more
authoritatively than I can hope to do.

Three points seem important in trying to assess the
power and persuasiveness of Becker's schematization of
modern European history. First, that history, as Becker
shaped it, was directly complementary to the national
history of the United States. Becker had come to European history in the first place in search of the roots of
the American revolution, and he never ceased to search
out other relationships that spanned the Atlantic. Not
surprisingly he found what he looked for, as we historians usually do.

Moreover, the manner in which Becker's kind of European history complemented that of the United States gave the European past a peculiar significance for Americans. Ideas and techniques that shaped American life came out of Europe; and the fact that they started there implied a longer history from which the wise might hope to profit. Europe, indeed, was like a mirror in which Americans could perhaps glimpse a simulacrum of their own future, or at least of one possible version of it. The view across the Atlantic might conceivably allow the New World to anticipate pitfalls and avoid some of the catastrophes of the Old; but only if we were wise enough, and Becker had little faith in such an eventuality. Nevertheless, Europe as warning against and/or pilot toward the American future was, it seems to me, a very large part of the attraction of European history as Becker presented it to my generation.

Another way of putting this is to say that Becker saw the United States as part of an Atlantic world whose headquarters remained on the European side of the ocean. Winds of change in Europe reached America only after a time lag. It therefore behooved us to watch Old Europe closely for early warnings of future dangers to the Republic. Hitler had yet to come to power when Becker's textbook came out; but the ensuing years made this interpretation of European history and its importance no less plausible. Quite the contrary: throughout the prewar decade and especially in 1939–41 when I was at Cornell, Europeans acted and we reacted, moving like sleepwalkers or as though hypnotized by the clash of arms and ideologies coming at us from the other side of the ocean.

A second aspect of Becker's way of presenting modern history was that he made France, not Britain, the protagonist. Britain's industrial revolution he subordinated to the democratic revolution—ruthlessly, just as he buried the Puritan revolution in the Age of Kings and Nobles. In doing this, Becker was presumably reacting against a snooty East coast style of Anglo-American filiopietism and a version of American and world history that made the constitutional adventures of English-speaking peoples the guiding thread of all modern history. Everyone else, in this view, suffered from a regrettable backwardness, to be overcome, if at all, by becoming more and more like virtuous New Englanders or imperial Britons as the case might be. By reaching instead towards Thomas Jefferson and the French, Becker altered the shape of American and European history so as to make more room for the populist mid-America from which he came. Assuredly, Great Britain was quite systematically—almost mischievously—dethroned in his book. After no fewer than four chapters devoted to the work of Napoleon III and Bismarck, for example, Becker spends a chapter tidying up around the margins. It shows, to quote the title, "How Political Liberty Prospered in Two Empires: Russia and Great Britain, 1830–1885"; and as the dates suggest, guess who lagged behind? Great Britain, of course, with manhood suffrage delayed until 1884! And an unsolved Irish problem to boot.

In the third place, I suggest that Becker democratized and broadened access to modern history, by secularizing it. He treated religion as no more than a trival residue, relegating frictions between Protestants, Catholics and Jews to the back burner—so far back as almost to disappear. Anti-semitism is scarcely referred to and the *Kulturkampf* gets all of twelve lines in his textbook, while the First Vatican Council and Papal infallibility are not mentioned at all! But the resolute secularism of Becker's *Modern History* may have helped Americans of Catholic and Jewish background to feel more fully at home in the "democratic, scientific and industrialized civilization"—to quote the subtitle Becker applied to the whole book—whose rise he chronicled. One can readily see how such a secularized study of modern history, and particularly of the eighteenth century Enlightenment, could act as a solvent to the sectarian stratification of American society in the early twentieth century; and I suppose that this was what attracted Gottschalk and Gershoy so powerfully to Becker's teaching and made them his faithful pupils. If so, this was another secret of Becker's success in shaping my generation's vision of that newly perceived entity—the transatlantic, European-American past.

If I am right in suggesting that Becker enlarged the geographical and sociological boundaries of the meaningful American past in these two directions, I now can recognize that my own effort to extend the base of European history to embrace Orthodox as well as Latin Christendom, and my even more reckless venture into world history ought to count as no more than a continuation of Becker's own effort to transcend the ethnocentric narrowness he inherited. So in rebelling against perceived inadequacies in Becker's viewpoint I remained in a larger sense true to his example, just as his eighteenth century philosophers, in rebelling against Christianity, remained true to their Christian heritage by finding meaning and pattern in human history.

This brings me to the second level of my interaction with Becker: the professional and fully conscious. For what I have hitherto tried to delineate remained quite hidden from me until a few months ago when I set out to explore the way in which I had actually "known" him. It is quite otherwise with the enthusiastic response provoked by my first reading of *The Heavenly City of the Eighteenth Century Philosophers,* and my no less affirmative reaction to his magnificent essay "Everyman His Own Historian." I also read Becker on *The Declaration of Independence* during my undergraduate years, though I cannot now tell in exactly what order nor in what precise context I first encountered these three works.

What I do remember, and believe to be true, is that Becker's pages implanted two key ideas in my consciousness which I have never since found any reason to alter. Others besides Becker undoubtedly played a part in shaping my mind on these matters. But it was his pellucid prose that made everything treacherously clear and thoroughly convincing.

The first of these notions is that absolute, eternal truth in history is unattainable because the historian himself shapes whatever it is that he finds out about the past, whether he wants to or not. Frankly, I cannot see why this proposition is not self-evident to every thinking person. Nor can I understand why we are not willing and ready to admit that a historian's thought, like everybody else's, is governed by the vocabularies he in-

herits, and by the interplay of experience and in-
terpretive schemes that make up the climate of opinion
that happens to surround him. This does not deprive
individuals of limited originality. Each of us has some
input into our particular climate of opinion which, indeed, consists of nothing more than the totality of messages we exchange with one another, day in and day
out. But private and personal innovation can only de-
part slightly from established norms without surren-
dering intelligibility and losing relevance to the
situation as perceived by others.

To be sure, human beings can and do establish self-
consistent conventions that permit us to make perfectly
true statements within limits of the conventions that
define the meanings of the symbols involved. Two and
two will always make four; and the most intricate dem-
onstrations of mathematics remain just as true as that
simple proposition so long as the symbolic manipulation involved conforms to the canons of logical consistency. But mathematical self-consistency cannot
apply to human affairs. A model of historical truth that
disregards the social function of words and the evolution of symbolic meanings across time seems to me—
well—silly. But if the world of symbols—what Teil-
hard de Chardin aptly christened the noosphere—
evolves along with the ecosphere; i.e., if there is cultural as well as biological evolution—and again that
proposition seems self-evident to me—then how can
we reasonably object to finding ourselves immersed in
those twin processes?

I must suffer from some sort of mental opaqueness in
this matter, for nearly everyone who has written about

Becker finds fault with his relativism and thinks him inconsistent in affirming the long-range value of democracy and liberal government during World War II, after having described the limitations of liberalism and the inaccessibility of absolute historical truth in earlier essays. I see no inconsistency at all. Personal choice and preference exist and are entirely legitimate. Becker never doubted that, as far as I can see. Moreover, outlooks change with circumstances, as Becker always insisted. Liberal democracy as practiced in the United States did indeed look different by 1944 or 1945 than it had in 1932 or 1933; and why should a thoughtful historian not say so? Is that inconsistent? I don't see it as such. Quite the contrary. It is the person who maintains unaltered judgments about public affairs under changed circumstances who is inconsistent, for he must either find new reasons for old opinions, or else cut off input from a changing world to keep from having to alter his views.

So far as I can see, therefore, Becker needs no defense against charges of inconsistency or of having exaggerated the force of climates of opinion in shaping historical writing. Instead of apologizing for our limitations—still less denying them—what historians ought to do is to celebrate the grandeur of our calling as mythographers. For myth-making is a high and serious business. It guides public action and is our distinctively human substitute for instinct. Good myths—that is, myths that are credible, because they are compatible with experience, and specific enough to direct behavior—are the greatest and most precious of human achievements. Why should we not aspire to make such myths? No nobler calling exists among human kind.

Once upon a time, people believed that truth was timeless. They therefore relied on poets, priests, and philosophers to explain how the world worked. Of late, evidence of the evolutionary character of the entire physical universe, as well as of human thought and institutions, has become overwhelming. Even the stars are now studied historically, and scientific theories are understood not to be absolute but paradigmatic—approaching truth as a limit perhaps, but never attaining complete adequacy to reality. Thus time has truly become all-devouring. Every intellectual discipline has become historical, and in two senses. First, each discipline evolves internally as new concepts and observations accumulate and interact. Second, its subject matter (whether physical, geological, biological, or human) also changes in *its* behavior across time. Two trajectories, therefore, each of them in motion: one of interacting symbols, the other of interacting entities; and each acting upon the other, time without end!

A complex, confusing picture no doubt; but one that, properly comprehended, is also exhilarating, especially to a historian. For who but he is fitted by training and predilection to comprehend such a scene? Who can better point to the important conjunctures, the main lines, the particular items in the totality of messages available to us that most reward conscious attention?

History has indeed become an imperial discipline in my lifetime. A few economists hold out for universals and stubbornly disregard evidence of temporal and spatial limitations to their equations. But they are becoming a lonely crowd when even astronomers have become historically minded, and compute the evolution of the universe in terms of perhaps no more than three star generations since the "Big Bang."

Simultaneously, specialized historians of science are busy providing a conscious past for all the disciplines, making the contemporary state of each intelligible in a new way. As a result, the social as well as the physical sciences will never be independent of history again, and the notion that truth develops and changes with time and place will be harder and harder to gainsay. This is no small alteration of the intellectual landscape to have occurred in a single lifetime. Moreover this historicizing of knowledge tends to reverse older patterns whereby history and the social "sciences" modeled themselves on physics and other natural sciences. All now tend to become historical, and, being an historical imperialist by temperament, as well as by conviction, I do not see how the trend can be reversed without a deliberate, conscious repudiation of the evidence.

Garden-variety historians have a somewhat less conspicuously imperial role to play, for we traditionally and appropriately confine ourselves to public affairs. But the effort to make group action intelligible is no small task, especially in an age when public identities are in flux, and when personal loyalties heave and crack in response to new patterns of communication and new sensibilities propagated via those communications.

Accordingly, we historians ought to aspire to be the protagonists of twentieth (and twenty-first) century efforts to refine and improve the accuracy and adequacy of one group's reactions to another. Burying ourselves in detail is not the way to achieve that mythopoeic dignity. Thinking carefully about the grand outlines of the human past *is* the way to respond to the needs of our time; and I very much wish that more of my colleagues were bolder in the attempt. Fear of error is craven; serious and sustained effort to take account of available evidence is a moral and intellectual duty; and to know that one's best effort will not suffice for all times and places is the beginning of wisdom.

I for one am glad that we will never so far escape the human condition as to know anything for sure and certain and forever. If we did, there would be nothing to do but repeat the truth—like Becker's undergraduates repeating extracts from those infamous lecture precis. But to make public identities and actions clear and conscious through sensitive study of the human past is a challenge to our best capacities, both intellectual and moral. Becker did his best to understand the world he lived in and argued that the only way to do it was historically. His heirs and successors should do likewise, knowing full well that others elsewhere and in times to come will see things differently. That does not mean the effort is not worth making. Giving up amounts to an abdication of intelligence, and despairs of humanity's future.

So much for point number one. The second idea that I gleaned from Becker's professional writing was similar: to wit, that reformers and revolutionaries retain older patterns of thought even when they are most eager to repudiate the old and affirm something new. As Becker put it, to fight one another, men must find common ground. Common ground is guaranteed by the cultural process itself, since what a rising generation rejects in the inherited wisdom goes a long way to define what it affirms. Even the most violent revolutionaries are, in this sense, prisoners of the past, bound to the climate of opinion created among humans by the communication networks that make us social. Indeed, the only way to escape the past would be to sever contact with everyone else—and that way lies madness.

Our inescapable immersion in a climate of opinion that is both changing and seamless, with no total disjunctions and no perfect continuities, also seems self-evident to me, once the idea had been clearly articulated and persuasively illustrated, as Becker did in his *Heavenly City of the Eighteenth Century Philosophers*. Peter Gay and others who criticized that essay so vigorously in the symposium of 1956, reproduced as *Carl Becker's Heavenly City Revisted*, simply puzzle me. Surely continuity and change are both to be expected in any historical situation. Becker was not the first to affirm *plus ça change, plus c'est la même chose;* and I suspect that the anonymous eighteenth-century Frenchman who first framed these words was not original when *he* said it, either.

Even when I was young, the proposition that Russian revolutionaries had changed human nature by abolishing private property in the means of production seemed unconvincing, though enthusiasts proclaimed it to be true. Today the continuity between old and new in all the great revolutions of modern times seems obvious, whether in France, Russia, or China. Revolutionaries' intentions have little to do with the matter. They, like the rest of us, can be radically mistaken, and sometimes are driven deliberately to disguise continuities that they find embarrassing.

The intentions and self-consciousness of the *philosophes* were no different, and should *not* be taken at face value. Their anti-clericalism was Catholic dogmatism turned inside-out—different, yet also the same. Quite unrevolutionary transmission of completely ordinary tradition—even historiographical tradition—follows the same pattern. My effort, earlier in this lecture, to delineate the difference and continuity between Carl Becker's practice of history and my own is a case in point. My differences with him, great as they once seemed, were really no more than a ripple in a common stream of discourse—discourse whose basic parameters were all inherited, by him as much as by me, and through great depths of time as well as across the gap of a single generation. That, quite simply, is what human culture *is*—that is how it is transmitted; that is how it shapes our lives by directing attention to some aspects of the world around us, while lumping the rest together as background noise to be disregarded.

In preparing this lecture I read far more widely in Becker's published works than ever before. I am old enough by now and have survived enough blips in our climate of opinion to be able to recognize how broad and deep are the things I share with him and with other Americans. The generational gap between us was not very wide. Continuity was far more significant than I realized before undertaking this probe into the past. Let me in closing, therefore, sum up that continuity, as I am now able to see it.

First, Becker was interested in big questions: liberty and equality, progress and power, freedom and responsibility; the pattern and meaning of the whole human adventure. Nothing less satisfied him any more than it does me. Historical scholarship that burrowed into detail and lost sight of the big picture distressed and irritated him. I find myself railing against the same penchant among my fellow historians. His professional writing exhibited a persistent widening of horizon in time and space: from the national scene to an Atlantic community, and from that Atlantic community to a global historiography which, of course, he only sketched lightly during the last decade of his life—exactly the time when I knew him and failed to comprehend the task he had set for himself. Alas and alack, that I could have been so blind, but so it was; and only now, some forty-three years too late, do I see how clearly he anticipated the globalism of my own intellectual aspiration.

Second is the conundrum of detachment. Becker was certainly detached, or gave that impression. At the same time, he was firmly committed to liberal values, and cared deeply for the welfare of the Republic. Detachment as an ideal is like truth as an ideal: both remain unattainable, as we can never escape from human limitations. Yet as I just argued, to strive for truth— the best available truth—is a noble calling. And to strive for detachment in the pursuit of truth seems to me no less noble for being persistently just beyond our reach.

Yet awareness of the limits of our powers in seeking truth and in detaching ourselves from personal and collective biases and emotions can have deplorable consequences. Cynics may argue that since historical or any other kind of truth is only self-serving myth, any myth will do as long as it is believed and acted on energetically. Activists will say that since detachment is unattainable, commitment and conscious propaganda are clearly superior since they at least get things done. Either view debases the life of the mind by denying it the dignity of being an end in itself. No man aspires to be a "running dog" of capitalism, after all; nor to fawn on any other sort of interest group, I should suppose. But if we cannot escape limitations of time, place, and cultural heritage, why try? Why not join the interests, whatever they may be, and write our histories accordingly?

It may indeed seem perverse to say Yes, we *are* human and therefore must always be part of a climate of opinion in which special interests play prominent and sometimes dominant roles, and at the same time say that nonetheless it is better to try to escape and rise above the limited perspective imposed by heritage and milieu. It is even more perverse, perhaps, to say so when one also realizes that if everyone became detached, society would collapse. Too many voices loudly proclaiming divergent personal and private views may simply paralyze public action. Becker was aware, more poignantly than most, of this possibility, yet he always

held to the path of detachment and exemplified its virtues more fully than most of us ever manage to do.

By now, it seems clear that the risks he recognized
were less destructive than he feared. New myths, offering effective guides to public action, emerged in this
country during World War II and have served us well
for the ensuing thirty years. We face new problems
now, not altogether unlike those of the 1930s. But we
can perhaps believe more serenely than Becker's generation could, that the survival value of societies that tol-
erate a more or less free exercise of the life of the mind
may turn out to be rather better than the alternative
offered by the rigidities of an official ideology imposed
by the police power of the state. Having conflicting
points of view in circulation may make adaptation to
changing circumstances a bit easier than when some
rigid orthodoxy has first to be bent or twisted to accommodate the new. Liberalism, in short, may have a
future analogous to its not inglorious past. All depends
on how well we manage to cultivate detachment *and*
insight, so as to repair old myths in the light of new
experience, and keep them somehow in workable condition, generation after generation.

I conclude, therefore, that despite the disappointment I felt in 1939–41 when I met Carl Becker on this
campus and listened to his voice for a total of, perhaps,
fifty to sixty hours, and in spite of the barriers to effective communication between us that then prevailed, I
can still lay claim to be his pupil, even if I was so in
spite of myself.

Insofar as I do differ from him, it was at least partly

because of Toynbee and Braudel, whom I also met—in more disembodied fashion—here at Cornell in those same years. My next lectures will explore how that happened.

# Nine

✳

*Arnold J. Toynbee*

A great virtue of the Cornell graduate program in history before the war was its informality. There were no graduate courses, and we were encouraged to sit in on undergraduate lecture courses only so long as we did not take the exams. Graduate seminars did meet, but of the three I attended, only Professor Laistner's expected a paper; and even that, if I may say so, was a perfunctory exercise, since he assigned the topic and defined the source we were to use—the *Corpus Inscriptionum Latinarum.* The result was lots of time on my hands; indeed, I have never had so much spare time before or since.

Cornell's relaxed rhythm of graduate study allowed me when first I came here to concentrate on tidying up questions left over from my year of M.A. work at Chicago. I had addressed myself to the ancient Mediterranean world under a program that prescribed courses in art history, philosophy, and history in equal proportions. My M.A. thesis, entitled *Herodotus and Thucy-dides: The Structure of their Histories,* had not exhausted problems emerging from that year of study; so in my first year at Cornell I wrote three lengthy essays for myself, one on Plato, one on Truth, and one on European agriculture to the year 1000. Instead of inquiring into things someone else defined for me, I was thus able to follow the dictates of my own spirit, and to an amazing degree.

This was the situation into which Toynbee's *A Study of History* intruded. I well remember first catching sight of those three volumes, bound in bright green, nestling at eye level in one of the bays of the White Library. It was a completely random encounter: the books still smelt of fresh print, and had never been used before. Nor did I have the slightest idea of the experience that lay before me when I took them down from the shelves. What could be more noncommittal than *A Study of History,* with an unknown name on the spine? But I was soon engrossed. An easy chair adorned the central bay of the White Library, some fifteen feet from the place in the shelves where I stumbled on the *Study,* and there I planted myself for the next two or three days to read Toynbee's volumes through in one gulp. That was all that was then available of the *Study.* Volumes 4–6 had been published in England in September 1939, but they had not yet reached the shelves of Cornell's library; and by the time they did so I was doing something else and remained unaware of their existence until after the war.

Only two or three times in my life have I been transported by reading a work of intellectual discourse. It often happens that imaginative literature can do this by inviting the reader to identify himself with characters in a poem, play, or novel. My reading of Toynbee was that kind of experience. But on this occasion I identified with another person's ideas, expressed abstractly and without the mediation of imaginary human characters. Nevertheless, for a while his thoughts were my thoughts—or so it seemed. Afterwards, letdown; more mundane experience flowed in; differences of outlook and sensibility obtruded; questions arose for me that Toynbee had not touched upon. But the moment of transport left its mark, as rapture always does. Older ideas required readjustment in my mind to make room for Toynbee, and conversely, Toynbee's ideas had to be twisted about so as to fit in with what I already knew and believed.

Only three years before, I had essayed Spengler, quite in vain. He had drawn on his classical training to sketch cycles of civilization similar to Toynbee's, but I could not comprehend Spengler's Germanic thought-world. What especially displeased me was the numerology that seemed to pervade tables at the back of Spengler's book where parallel phases of each civilization were laid out into precisely equivalent temporal segments. Such mechanical exactitude does not accord with the imprecision of human interaction. It did not convince me then and does not convince me now. Why, then, should Toynbee's civilizations with their patterned sequence of genesis, growth, breakdown, and dissolution have attracted me so powerfully three years afterwards, in 1939?

First of all, Toynbee's vocabulary was English

whereas Spengler's ideas were dressed in a heavy armor of Germanic abstractions that were entirely uncongenial to an American undergraduate. But the really decisive factor, it seems to me now, was the public experience of the late 1930s, dominated by an obvious drift toward the war that actually broke out in the fall of 1939, just as I began my studies at Cornell. In 1938 I had pored over the pages of Thucydides for my master's thesis. His speeches then had nearly the same effect on me as they had had for Toynbee in 1914, when he, too, found pregnant echoes of contemporary experience in the ancient historian's pages. This Thucydidean magic was not merely personal and idiosyncratic. Elmer Davis, a well-known journalist who later became head of the Office of War Information, had this to say in 1939: "*Mein Kampf* and what else? There are plenty of other books that offer illumination but . . . if you can find time for only one book—one book to help you understand the times we live in . . . you might as well pass by all the moderns and read Thucydides."[1]

During my last year at Chicago, therefore, I had been sensitized to the remarkable echo between ancient Greek political patterns and those of my own day. Indeed, I had decided to write a book that would explore that echo by pursuing the cyclic pattern that apparently prevailed in classical and in more modern European history. That was why, after my year of classical study at Chicago, I wanted to do a year of medieval history with Carl Stephenson and then go on to modern Europe with

1. Elmer Davis, "Required Reading," *Saturday Review of Literature,* 14 October 1939, p. 4.

Becker. But now, all of a sudden, I met a man who had
been that way before me; who had explored the implications of the Thucydidean echo with a dazzling virtuosity, taking on all the world and making sense not
just of European but of world history by applying the
Thucydidean pattern to all the civilizations of the
earth. No wonder I was dazzled! Here was a fellow spirit soaring far beyond the limits of my own knowledge
and experience. A giant in the earth! An authentic hero
of the lamp! A historian whose tragic vision of the limits of human capacity for civilization resonated strongly
with a general sense of imminent disaster generated by
the onset of World War II.

Another dimension of the first volume of Toynbee's
*A Study of History* deserves emphasis. The classical, specifically Thucydidean vision of an ineluctable cycle in
human affairs emphasized impersonal process acting on
a plane that overrode human wills and intentions. History as a record of what men said and did was all very
well; full of sound and fury, to be sure, and signifying
perhaps a bit more than Shakespeare's nothing, but not
much more. Purposes that always fail of realization
soon seem trivial; hopes betrayed merely foolish. A
wise and knowledgeable historian might therefore
hope, like Thucydides, to penetrate behind the screen
of what men said and did to what really happened; that
is, to the pattern of interaction that bound humanity's
struggling atoms into an intelligible whole that was
both less and more than its parts. Less because all the
piquant human details were filtered out; more, because
such a pattern, once seen and understood, could make
the frustration of individual and collective intentions

more nearly bearable. Such is the consolation of philosophy—since ancient times a reasonably adequate substitute for faith.

God's inscrutable will acting through divine providence was the traditional explanation of the perennial gap between human expectation and actual experience. Historians of the nineteenth century, however, had been eager to leave God out of history by concentrating on the superficial level of things said and done—especially those which happened, by custom and by chance, to get recorded in government archives. As long as the world moved on lines basically acceptable to middle-class heirs of Latin Christian civilization this was a generally satisfactory posture. Archives could be made to reveal a great deal about the rise of national states, and this was the primary focus of interest for the new "scientific" history that made its way into academic institutions, first in Germany, then in other European countries, and from the 1880s in this country too. Even if reasons for the rise of Germany, Britain, France, or the United States to greatness remained a mystery and a faith—indeed especially since that was so—historians could cheerfully puzzle out details, leaving the beneficence of the pattern as a whole to take care of itself. But when unacceptable and destructive human behavior came to the fore—what then? World Wars I and II made that question far from academic in the twentieth century. Precisely the same question had confronted Thucydides in the fifth century B.C. when Athens's imperial greatness came a cropper. No wonder he spoke so powerfully across the centuries!

For Thucydides, as for Toynbee and myself, simple

reaffirmation of older views was unattractive. A God or gods who intervened inscrutably in human history seemed too facile an explanation of the vanity of human wishes. The natural philosophers of Ionia, like the world machine erected so pridefully by modern scientists, left no obvious room for Providence. Simply to invoke an unknowable divine will therefore looked like intellectual abdication. So did the molelike diligence of professional historians who busied themselves in archives to avoid thinking about the big and urgent questions of a new age. Presumably there were sophists in Athens after 431 B.C. who continued to teach as before, refusing to recognize that the values of Periclean Athens had reached a crisis. But Plato and Thucydides saw and felt and thought otherwise; and the two of them could therefore speak to an age whose own inherited values and ways of life were adrift in very much the same fashion as had been the case in ancient Athens. Becker and Toynbee belonged with Plato and Thucydides in this respect, for they saw that the liberal compromise of the nineteenth century had worn itself out. Both worried about it intensely, and to my youthful mind in 1939, Toynbee's answers seemed better than Becker's questions. I responded accordingly.

Exculpation is perhaps expected on a campus where the ghost of Carl Becker still walks. Let me therefore make the further observation that in swallowing Toynbee whole—or nearly whole—I did not entirely reject Becker's quizzical uncertainty. In particular, I was able to recognize that Toynbee's view of civilization as a work of art that conformed to the structure of Greek tragedy was no more than a secularized version of an older faith. Frances Cornford's *Thucydides Myth-historicus* had convinced me of the religious motif that lay behind the great Athenian's structuring of his book about the Peloponnesian war. Hubris and Ate, pride and destructive rashness, acting as depersonalized substitutes for the gods of Olympus, were not notably more accessible to human understanding than was the Will of God as Augustine had spelled it out in the Christian tradition. Indeed, Hubris and Ate, acting rather more mechanically than God's will, were in logic a rather less adequate theoretical undergirding for explaining the variety of human encounters with the world. But Toynbee's cycle had, or seemed to have, adequacy to the immediate experience of the 1930s, when peoples and governments drifted toward a war that no one wanted, foreseeing all the while that disaster was bound to ensue. A machinery that could compel conscious sleepwalking seemed needed. The structured pattern of Toynbee's cycle of civilization, with its ready-made niche for the wars of the twentieth century, therefore answered a felt need and made the leap of faith easy for me, even though I half recognized its kinship to the other leap toward Christian faith which I boggled at making.

Cycling through history with the ancients as generalized and brought up to date by Toynbee resonated with two other aspects of my mind. One I hardly know how to estimate, for no one ever attempted to teach me Calvinist theology, or get me to accept the doctrine of predestination. Nevertheless, in my youth I had strong affinity for the notion of a closed universe, whose future was foreordained by its past. I felt an elevation of spirit

in thinking of myself and all around me as part of a
hurtling process that far transcended human will and
consciousness; a process that submerged humanity,
earth, solar system and galaxy, and the universe itself
in cosmic change whose lines may well have fixed from
the moment of the Big Bang and whose future, however unclear to us, was as certain as its past. Acting in
ignorance of the outcome then becomes free and easy;
or can be, since no one is responsible for the way things
turn out. What will be, will be. One simply does the
best one can and hopes, expecting to be surprised—
favorably or unfavorably—by the event. Freedom, in
short, can quite genuinely arise from conscious submission to the constraints of a world historical process.
For, as all the great religions have discovered, personal
abasement, paradoxically, permits personal aggrandize-
ment. Even an infinitesimal atom, adrift in a cosmic
process, is, if it also knows its place, consciously shar-
ing in something truly great!

These paradoxes, buried deep in the Christian tradition and raised to special prominence by John Calvin,
assuredly informed my mind, and inclined me to accept
Toynbee's vision of the cycle of civilizations. Similar
resonances, I am sure, prepared a large number of
Americans to respond to Toynbee after World War II,
when his book became generally available in 1947 in its
condensed version.

A taste for predestination may have emanated from
my cradle—who knows? But another cluster of ideas
that attracted me to A Study of History clearly came
from my undergraduate encounter with cultural anthropology as conceived by Robert Redfield and others

of his generation. When I listened to his lectures in 1937, Redfield was trying to work out a general typology for human societies by utilizing simple variables that would nevertheless fit all the enormous variety of actual human communities to be found on the face of the earth. By comparing a remote rural community in Yucatan with a neighboring village more in touch with the outside world, Redfield had noted that the realm of sacred, collective, and cohesive behavior diminished as one approached the urban center of the peninsula at Merida, where secularization, individualization, and fragmentation of cultural behavior into discrepant parts reached a sort of metropolitan climax. Redfield suggested that these three variables, distinguishing civilized from folk societies, might have general diagnostic value, allowing an observer to locate any and every actual human community somewhere along the spectrum.

That was exciting enough; but it was easy for an aspiring historian to extend the scheme still further by imagining a temporal dimension, and to find, in doing so, cycles of rise and fall analogous to those Toynbee described. One had merely to suppose that the three traits Redfield recognized as characteristic of civilization had psychic limits which, if transgressed, would lead to social breakdown. Perhaps consensus was bound to fail sooner or later in civilized societies, whenever the garment of the sacred became too threadbare to cushion collisions among social classes and other interest groups. Thucydides's case study could be assimilated to such a scheme—consider his account of class war in Corcyra! Perhaps the problems of the 1930s, in

echoing Thucydides so ominously, portended breakdown as brutal as that which had occurred in the Greek
world of the fifth century B.C. Perhaps, indeed, a proper perspective on humanity's historical experience
would show that civilization itself was a sort of cultural
disease, a fitful fever provoked when the human penchant for weaving a coherent pattern of culture met
with defeat because of too many changes, too much
buffeting from outside, too many strangers within the
gates, too little time to reduce novelties to routine and
ritual.

Consensus certainly seemed strained in civilized
countries of the western world in the 1930s; and before
reading Toynbee my flirtation with Redfield and
Thucydides had already convinced me that a suitably
bold projection of the very latest social science upon the
historical record might well produce a cycling pattern
that could explain the uncanny echoes that resounded
for a twentieth-century reader from the ancient Athenian's pages. Obviously, Toynbee had not read Ralph
Linton, Ruth Benedict, Robert Redfield, and the other
cultural anthropologists who nourished my mind, nor
was he significantly in touch with the other social sciences—not even with Marx, who pervaded so much
thinking in the 1930s. I could therefore hope to but-
tress the edifice Toynbee had erected by bringing concepts of cultural anthropology in particular, and of
contemporary social science in general, to bear on the
historical phenomenon of civilizational cycles. Humili-
ty, clearly, was not my long suit. Yet for a young man
wanting to make sense of the world and who, unlike

Toynbee, had been inoculated with the virus of American social science, what other path was there to pursue?

This, then, so far as I can reconstruct the circumstances of more than forty years ago, was why Toynbee's *A Study of History* so entranced me. He opened new vistas, previously beyond my ken. Civilizations I had never considered before became—so to speak—visible for the first time. Obviously, the existence of China, Japan, India, Islam, and of Africa and pre-Columbian America was not news to me in 1939; yet their histories had never seemed legitimate or necessary objects of curiosity. Even eastern Europe had remained an unknown land, bristling with unpronounceable names and unintelligible details, until I came to Cornell. How much more impenetrable were Asia, Africa, and pre-Columbian America! Yet Toynbee had not quailed at the task of trying to understand them all. It was both heartening and sobering to see how much more there was to be thought about than I had previously imagined. For it was now clear to me that the book I had earlier envisioned that would anatomize the ancient and modern European patterns of rise and fall was not enough. I, too, like Toynbee, would have to think about humanity as a whole and explore the histories of peoples and places totally unknown to me.

In retrospect, I find it amazing to remember how completely my education had excluded the vast majority of humankind from any sort of attention. Even in the 1930s, Japan had begun to challenge the Eurocentric vision of the globe. European empire over Asia and Africa was already wearing thin. Realization that ancient cultures and civilizations retained an enormous power over human behavior ought to have been apparent to any reflective person who read about Gandhi's successful defiance of the British Raj. But absolutely nothing of this seismic movement reached University of Chicago classrooms. My teachers evaded the issue totally by paying no attention to any part of the world outside of Europe and English-speaking North America. The smug belief that backward peoples would sooner or later catch up and become civilized, just like us, had indeed been shaken by the savagery of World War I, followed by the failure of the Wilsonian recipe of self-determination to solve the world's problems. But my teachers remained oblivious. The curriculum was built on the unspoken assumption that an acquaintance with our European cultural roots, extended back to ancient Greece and Rome, but no farther, was all that mattered.

I can therefore attest that the beginning of wisdom with respect to the global scope of the meaningful past came to me here at Cornell by reading Toynbee. Spengler had failed to convince me that other civilizations were worth thinking about; *A Study of History* awakened me from that dogmatic slumber once and for all. This, I suppose, is the deepest debt I owe to Arnold Joseph Toynbee and I am proud to acknowledge it. In addition, his notion of a plurality of civilizations within the confines of the European continent shed light on my concern to understand the difference between Russian and west European history. And if, as Toynbee declared, the Ottoman empire represented still a third civilization, then Balkan crosscurrents took on new

meaning as well. I have found this idea helpful ever since in approaching the history of eastern and southeastern Europe. Here, too, I owe an enduring debt to Toynbee's insights.

Then, in the summer of 1941, the war caught up with me. Drafted into the army, I was in due season assigned to Greece, where I had a chance to see that ancient land and to study its people in a time of extreme hardship and political crisis, 1944–46. Oddly enough my experience in Greece closely paralleled Toynbee's youthful encounter with Greek peasants on the eve of the first Balkan war. I, too, visited remote mountain villages and decided that the political future of that country rested on what happened in those poverty-stricken rural communities whence come the guerrilla fighters of modern Greek history. Toynbee's search for Homeric survivals in 1911–12 and my encounters with real, live guerrilla bands a generation afterwards acquainted us both with a world vastly different from that which we had grown up to; confronted us, in fact, with representatives of a different civilization—Greek Orthodox peasants in all their glory!—lively, curious, hospitable, even at a time when their customary ways of life were in what turned out, in the 1940s, to be a final, truly mortal crisis.

In Greece I also met my wife, whose father had been Toynbee's walking companion through Greece in 1911. Thanks to her I actually met the great man himself in April, 1947, a few weeks after *Time Magazine* had made him famous overnight with a cover story that packaged the ideas of *A Study of History* for the American public. My first sight of him therefore was of an elderly Englishman, whose accent I had difficulty in comprehending, rocking gently on a Kentucky veranda deep in conversation with his old friend. At odd moments during the next few days he scribbled away with a stubby pencil at an article for *Life,* Henry Luce's other mass circulation magazine. In its way, that meeting was as exotic as my encounters with Greek guerrillas had been, and as memorable.

The storm of publicity generated in this country by Henry Luce's enthusiasm for Toynbee's ideas was then in full spate. A fateful new constellation of public affairs, symbolized by the Truman doctrine of March, 1947, lay behind Toynbee's sudden fame, for in the spring of 1947 the Grand Alliance of World War II fell apart—definitively. All the wartime hopes for a peaceful postwar world were in disarray. Events defied the wishes and expectations of the American public. Good will and the hope-filled rhetoric of the United Nations had become irrelevant. A pattern of behavior independent of anyone's intention was again manifesting its power—over us and over the Russians, over everyone, everywhere in the world.

Was not western civilization caught in the throes of a time of troubles, working its way toward a universal state as prescribed by the Toynbeean cycle of civilization? Henry Luce, another ex-Calvinist, clearly thought so. The only question was whether it would be an American or a Russian empire; and this, I think, was what he expected Mr. Toynbee to proclaim in the article for *Life* whose topic had been prescribed as "The Prospect for America," or something to that effect. But

Toynbee balked at prophecy and declined to make the future clear. Perhaps for that reason, the editors of *Life* never published his essay. I suspect that Toynbee remembered that during World War I he had lent his pen to propaganda of which he later became much ashamed, and realized in 1947 that he might again become a cat's-paw for men who were seeking to influence public opinion, if need be at the expense of sober truth.

Toynbee said nothing in my presence to support this surmise; but his casual insouciance in meeting a deadline for *Life* and his capacity to take a lively interest in the scene around him much impressed me. We visited an old buffalo salt lick in the Knobs, and having lost our way, tried to get directions from hillbillies whose reaction to strangers was far more timorous and hostile than anything to be met with in the Greek mountains. Toynbee the traveler obviously found Kentucky quite as interesting as Greece or any other place where his discerning eye could recognize traces of the past in a landscape that could be counted on to outlast its current human occupants far into the future. To see a segment of America scrutinized in such a way was novel experience for me. I had done something of the kind in Greece; here was a man turning the spotlight of historical and geographical consciousness on my own back yard, and finding it quite as interesting as I had found exotic lands overseas. The more one knows, the more one sees and understands; and Toynbee did indeed know a lot about how human beings had lived at different times and in different parts of the earth. Travel

sharpened his senses. I have never met a better travel-
ing companion with whom to share reactions to a landscape and its human inhabitants.

As a result of my Kentucky meeting with Toynbee,
he invited me to spend two years in London at Chatham
House, 1950–52, writing a volume in the wartime
survey of international relations which he edited. During those two years I saw him nearly every working
day, and talked with him at teatime not only about the
progress of my work and of Chatham House affairs generally, but also about his own effort to complete the
final volume of *A Study of History*. That task consumed
his morning hours. Afternoons were devoted to his editorial duties at Chatham House, evenings to reading
ahead for the *Study*. It was a rigorous regimen no
doubt, but he drove ahead, inspired by the deadline of
his retirement, due in 1954, and the simultaneous exp-
iry of a grant from the Rockefeller Foundation which
financed both his personal research and the Chatham
House survey during his final years as director of studies for the Royal Institute of International Affairs.

In accepting the invitation to work at Chatham
House I had a sense that I was going to sit at the feet of
a master. In crossing the ocean to associate with
Toynbee, I hoped to prepare myself for writing the big
book I had projected ever since my undergraduate days.
I am not sure what I expected to learn, perhaps how to
write world history, or perhaps I only expected to test
and clarify my organizing ideas through private conversation and daily intercourse with the man who had so
fired my imagination eleven years before.

I did indeed find out how Toynbee wrote his book.

His practice was to read for several hours each evening, gathering ideas and information to use in the remaining sections of the *Study*. To bridge the gap between the time of reading and the time of writing, Toynbee relied on notebooks in which he wrote down whatever seemed significant to him in what he had just read. He relied on summary notes, rather than bothering with painstaking transcriptions of the *ipssisima verba,* as I had been taught was necessary for scholarly accuracy. If the exact words became important he could look them up later, and in the meantime, he lightened the labor of transcription enormously by recording only the gist.

Toynbee declared that he found it helpful to let a few weeks or even years elapse between the time he read a book and the time he might wish to refer to it in his writing. His notebooks became quarries from which references and instances, parallels, and turns of phrases could be extracted as needed for the unfolding texture of *A Study of History.* Things read yesterday were too raw to be properly incorporated into the structure of his thought. He needed at least six weeks by his own calculation for the new matter to shake down, so to speak, and fit itself into the landscape established by the general pattern of his mind.

His method of work encouraged me to try a more radical experiment. For in writing my own book at Chatham House on the diplomatic relations of Britain, America and Russia, 1941–46, I improved on Toynbee's practice by refraining from taking any notes at all. The various memoirs on which I depended were not so numerous that they could not all be piled on one desk. Newspaper clippings that constituted the other prin-

cipal source were available from the Chatham House
library in cartons presorted by subject, which could
also be piled high around the typewriter where I
worked. By reading as fast as possible, the matter of the
next chapter could then take form within four or five
weeks; whereupon it became possible to make an outline and start to compose, referring to the original
sources as needed from memory.

Emancipation from notetaking was, indeed, the
great discovery of my time at Chatham House. To take
a note one must first know what is important; but that
is knowable only after the shape and meaning of the
subject to be inquired into has begun to emerge from
the mists enshrouding it at the start. If there are no
mists, the subject is not really worth pursuing. But
until one knows what is important, how can one take
notes? Total transcription is wasteful, even when the
xerox machine makes it easy; and hours of xeroxing,
like hours of industrious notetaking, can be used to put
off the serious task of making sense of the matter at
hand. Notetaking has the further disadvantage of slow-
ing down the pace at which one can read, so that more
is forgotten by the time the reluctant thinker does get
around to worrying about the shape and meaning of his
subject.

I suspect that the triviality of much of our professional history writing arises from the fetish of notetaking. By choosing a subject close to what others have
written about so that the points of debate have already
been defined, a historian can indeed know in advance
what is worth transcribing onto a notecard. With suitable diligence, he or she can readily accumulate a thick

wad of notes and write a monograph that contributes to the state of the art by adding a few instances that either support or, more commonly, fail to conform to what other historians have found. Endless revisionism and increasing triviality result. Who cares, other than another historian whose Ph.D. dissertation or latest monograph touches on the same or some closely adjacent field?

To be sure, research emancipated from notetaking requires its own kind of diligence and an active memory—the kind that persistently sorts out the wheat from the chaff, and fastens on what matters as soon as a meaningful landscape starts to emerge from the fog of initial ignorance. This is not nearly as risky as it may sound to someone who has never tried to read and think without bothering to record as he goes along. I find that I can remember whatever turns out to be interesting and important for a period of about six weeks. Beyond that length of time, I forget about as much as I can pick up by fresh reading. By looking at the most promising materials first, therefore, I can be reasonably confident that after six weeks further effort will merely decrease the likelihood of thinking clearly and to good effect. But by spending all available waking hours at the task, and by skimming repetitious material, one can, I assure you, get through a lengthy bibliography in six weeks!

A research procedure that eliminates notetaking allows the inquirer to concentrate on big questions. Entrancing vistas can open before such an attack, at least sometimes. In particular, breakneck reading facilitates cross-fertilization of conventional compartments of learning by making accessible the perspective of a high-flying airplane as against the worm's eye view. I do not mean to imply that one form of thought can replace the other. Rather, a vigorous republic of learning requires persistent interaction between generalizing vision and detailed information. Detail, after all, gets its meaning through connection with some overarching pattern, and the pattern achieves persuasiveness only by accommodating an indefinite population of details.

Chatham House and Toynbee's example therefore served me well, and did prepare me, as I had hoped might be the case, for writing the big book I aspired to. Two years after getting back from Chatham House, I was able to begin work on *The Rise of the West: A History of the Human Community*. Ten years later I finished. In all that time I never took a note, and only rarely—not more than half a dozen times in all—was I unable to find a passage I wanted to cite. It is an emancipation I heartily recommend to others who wish to write more general history than is encouraged by our habit of taking notes.

In other ways my two years with Toynbee at Chatham House were not as stimulating as I had expected. I made some tentative efforts to interest him in cultural anthropology, but he was unresponsive. My thoughts about the importance of technology seemed trivial to him. My suggestion that civilizations interacted constantly with one another, and not only under special conditions such as renaissances, apparentation and affiliation, etc., as he had decided—led to oddly inconclusive discussions. In this and other instances, Toynbee acknowledged my point, expressed interest in it, but when pressed, reaffirmed his older view on the matter under discussion.

Having now surpassed Toynbee's age as it was in 1952, I am better able to sympathize with his reaction to my probing than I was thirty years ago. I can see now that it was too late for him to reconsider the edifice he had erected. Given the enormous response his ideas had generated in the United States and elsewhere—his quasi-apotheosis in Japan was still ahead when I knew him in 1952—it would have been strange indeed for him to have escaped feeling that he had discovered something too valuable to be tampered with lightly. Nevertheless, his habitual courtesy and genuine kindness to young whippersnappers like myself impelled him to listen intently and say "yes, yes" to whatever it was I might say without taking my remarks seriously.

Our paths had, in fact, diverged markedly. He had abandoned his classical frame of mind. Serious personal stresses, climaxing in a powerful mystical experience that occurred in 1939, convinced him of the existence of a supernatural reality which he soon felt able to refer to familiarly as God. History indeed became the record of God's self-revelation to humanity; and civilizations became instruments whose recurrent breakdown sensitized men to the supernatural, and thereby propelled humanity forward towards a more perfect knowledge of God. It was an Augustinian view, generated by personal disappointment and suffering more acute than anything Augustine records in his *Confessions*. Yet the odd thing was that Toynbee's change of mind about the meaning of human experience did not dissuade him from completing the original, pagan plan of *A Study of*

*History,* even though parts of it as originally projected simply ceased to interest him. Perhaps he felt it a duty to complete a monument to the times in which he lived. I also think that he felt himself to be no more than a mote in the grand panorama of humanity's encounter with God. The great work, which he had privately referred to in earlier years as his "Nonsense Book," may often have seemed to him no more than an object of amused condescension, whose errors and inadequacies were beyond repair, if only because he himself was tired of it and interested now in other things.

This is pure speculation. At the time I was puzzled by his apparent illogic in both accepting and rejecting criticism. He carried this habit to an extreme in volume 8, part of which he gave me to read in manuscript. I made a number of suggestions, expecting him to reflect on my remarks, and then alter a few passages in light of what I had to say, while rejecting the rest. Instead he printed extracts from my commentary as footnotes, without altering his original text in any jot or tittle! I was taken aback, for I had not tried to express a balanced point of view, and picked only on points of difference.

This surprisingly slapdash procedure attested the fact that Toynbee was eager to finish, and could not afford to delay the completion of the ten volumes by questioning the fundaments upon which the *Study* rested. Even the fact that his own beliefs had altered radically did not stop him; how much the less could observations coming from outside deflect him from his goals?

The result therefore of two years of Toynbee's company was to make clear how much our paths had begun to diverge. For I, too, like him, was ready to abandon cycling through history. The cumulative character of human skills and knowledge and the persistent human bias for improving on devices that satisfied ordinary, vulgar wants seemed more important to me than repetitive patterns of political interaction among states, though the existence of such patterns seemed to me then, as it does still, to be an important phenomenon. But it was a phenomenon of less commanding significance than I had thought in the 1930s; or so the outcome of World War II and the new lease on life that managed economies offered to liberal society convinced me.

But the aspect of human life on which my attention fastened—the technological, material and ecological—was the polar opposite from what had come to interest Toynbee. Reaching toward God, he aspired toward the empyrean. I was reaching downward, digging in dusty earth, wishing to understand how flows of matter and energy sustain human lives, and make us uniquely powerful among living species. One of the things drawing me downward was the French *Annaliste* tradition of which Braudel is the most distinguished representative. In my next lecture, I will therefore explore the way in which I became entangled in that tradition during my student days at Cornell, and analyze the game of tag I have played with Braudel since first I became aware of his work some twenty-five years ago.

Yet in justice to Toynbee, let me say that near the very end of his life, he interested himself afresh in the material setting of human life, and also expanded his sensitivity from literary to visual evidences of the past. The title of his posthumous book, *Mankind and Mother Earth,* points in that direction, though it was only a feeble sketch—feeble and far, far more prolix than Becker's unwritten sketch of a universal historiography. Perhaps, therefore, Toynbee listened more truly than at first appeared to what I and others had to say, carrying it all in his heart until, in the fullness of time, he could get round to considering it in earnest. But by the time he, too, turned earthwards, his life was near its end and his powers had decayed, preventing him from achieving what he had projected.

That failure ought not to detract from appreciation of his achievement. To have noticed that the world was really round by taking seriously the history of other peoples in trying to understand our own was no small feat; and this Arnold J. Toynbee did for the English-speaking world for the first time. For a while, his reputation far outran that of other historians of the twentieth century and then collapsed as rapidly as it had risen. Now, thirty-five years after Henry Luce first launched Toynbee on the American scene, it is time to discard the tinsel of those times and give Toynbee his due. For me, at least, he ranks with Carl Becker as one of the principal shapers of my mind, a historian whose magnificent boldness deserves more of admiration and of imitation than the historical profession has yet been willing to accord him.

# Ten

## *Fernand Braudel*

My encounter with Fernand Braudel was of a different
kind from those I have discussed hitherto. I first met
him personally in 1968, having discovered his magnificent work on the Mediterranean about a decade earlier
while working on my own book, *The Rise of the West*.
But by then my mind was made up on all important
questions, so I merely plundered Braudel's pages for
matter that interested me, as a check of my footnotes
will show.

All the same, in reading his book for the first time I
recognized a kindred spirit, inasmuch as the French
school of thought, of which Braudel represents the
finest flower, had been important in shaping my own
approach to history. But my initiator into the *Annaliste*
thought-world was the medievalist, Marc Bloch,
whereas Fernand Braudel apprenticed himself to Lucien
Febvre, Bloch's friend and coeditor of the *Annales* when
that periodical was new and when they both were pro-

fessors at the University of Strasbourg after World War I. So my relation to Braudel and the *monde Braudellien* was fraternal rather than filial, inasmuch as we both were trying to expand upon our heritages, some small part of which we held in common.

My exploration of the French *Annaliste* tradition of learning was the indirect result of my first indiscretion as a graduate student: the act of actually reading a book written in a foreign language. This occurred in 1938 when I sat down one day with Franz Cumont's slender volume, *Comment la Belgique fut romanisée*. I am a miserable linguist and had always before approached foreign language texts with dictionary in hand to look up the words I did not know. This time I was hurried and unsure whether Cumont could tell me anything needed for a paper I had to write. So I just started in and kept on going without bothering to look up unknown words or to puzzle out passages that remained opaque on first inspection. The type was large, the paper sumptuously thick, as befitted the pre-World War I Royal Belgian Academy, and Cumont's 120 pages turned easily. So after two or three hours I was through. And behold, I knew what he had said, at least in a general way. Amazing! Like a nestling's first flight! Something I had always known ought to happen had happened: I had made sense of Cumont's prose without translating a single word.

But there was a second aspect to this experience. For in reading about tiny, isolated Roman settlements along the lower reaches of the Scheldt and Meuse Rivers, I became vividly aware of the contrast between the forested expanses that Cumont described, punctuated only by swamps and waterlogged plains, and the smiling fields and bustling cities of medieval Flanders and Brabant. Clearly, something happened between the first centuries of the Christian era and the twelfth-thirteenth, when the Low Countries became the most active seat of commercial life north of the Alps. The Dark Ages, however inimical to good Latin, must have witnessed a remarkable advance to make such a difference; and in a vague way I wondered why Roman populations had left the rich plains of Belgium so completely uncultivated.

There was, of course, a received version of medieval economic history in the 1930s. It percolated down to me as the "Pirenne thesis." As mediated by textbooks and my not-too-reliable recollection, that thesis ran about as follows: in Merovingian times, trade links with the eastern Mediterranean remained alive and the continuity of Frankish with Roman Gaul was therefore stronger than earlier historians had supposed. Pirenne thus postponed the Dark Ages to the Carolingian era, when the Moslems' conquest of the Levant and North Africa gave them control of the Mediterranean seaways, thus cutting off contact between Gaul and the more developed lands of the eastern Mediterranean. The Arabs, therefore, compelled the Frankish state and society to rely on more strictly local resources, thereby transferring the center of gravity of Frankland from the Mediterranean coastlands to the Rhine.

Pirenne had come to this view, I believe, largely on the basis of a new sort of evidence: the distribution of coin finds, which diminished markedly both in quantity and quality after about A.D. 650. Yet Pirenne's evidence did not prevent me from wondering whether religious animosity really did suffice to sever trade. Venice and Genoa, a few centuries later, had not boggled at exchanging goods with infidels; and if Moslems traded with Christians in the eleventh and twelfth centuries, why not in the seventh and eighth as well?

These then were questions and doubts I brought with me to Cornell in 1939. Carl Stephenson, whom I assisted in my first year, was a pupil of Pirenne's, and always spoke of the Belgian scholar with reverence. Questioning the adequacy of the Pirenne thesis was therefore not quite comme il faut in his seminar; and since our topic for the year was the origin of feudalism, I had no occasion to do so anyway. Stephenson asked the members of his seminar to read the principal works he had already consulted in preparing an article on feudalism which he subsequently published in the *American Historical Review*.[1] Each of us was assigned a book. Mine was Georg Waitz, *Deutsche Verfassungsgeschichte,* all eight volumes thereof. Threading my way through thousands of pages of heavy academic German was a hard way to find out that Waitz thought feudalism was a Roman and not a Germanic institution. But that was my task. Stephenson already knew what he had found significant in each of the works he assigned to us, and presumably used his seminar as a kind of check, to see whether we might by some chance turn up something he needed to think about before submitting his essay for publication. So far as I know,

1. Carl Stephenson, "The Origin and Significance of Feudalism," in *American Historical Review,* 46 (1941), pp. 788–812.

nothing new did crop up. Our oral reports on what we
had read limped along from week to week, prodded
toward the appropriate conclusion by Stephenson's
leading questions.

Nevertheless, early in the year the name of Marc
Bloch came to my attention. Feudalism, after all, had
some connection with manorialism, so Stephenson directed me to Bloch's *Les Caractères originaux de l'histoire
rurale française*, published, oddly, in Oslo in 1931.
After Waitz, Bloch's prose was like a draught of cool
water in a dry and thirsty land. Not only did Bloch
write French, which I could read much more easily
than that other language from across the Rhine; he also
got right down to earth, describing how real people
made a living from the land. Bloch's rural France smelt
of the barnyard, not of dusty archives. His archival and
philological learning was quite as impressive as that of
his German predecessor, but he carried it so lightly
that not erudition but the everyday flavor of peasant life
oozed from his pages. The legalisms that preoccupied
Waitz's attention were conspicuous for their absence.
(What Waitz was really trying to figure out was how
German national sovereignty got so mysteriously mis-
laid during the middle ages that Bismarck had to re-
store it in the nineteenth century. No doubt I do the
German scholar an injustice in thus traducing him, but
I was not brave enough to consult his book again in
preparing this lecture and so permit my memory to
malign his motivation.)

Bloch, on the other hand, set out to describe how
France was actually cultivated from the time when natural forests and grasslands were first supplanted by

man-made fields and pastures until modern (mainly post-1789) changes began to alter traditional rural routines. He was concerned with differences between hill and plain, between north and south, and wherever significant contrasts in modes of exploiting the natural features of the landscape were discernible. That remarkable sensitivity to human geography and to the different ways human beings adjust their lives to varying landscapes, for which Braudel is so justly famous, was thus forefigured in Bloch's book, and in a masterful fashion.

The most marvelous aspect of the book was that Bloch used abundant local detail to bring out a fundamental distinction between a Mediterranean style of cultivation, which used a light plow that simply broke up the soil without turning it over, and a northern style of agriculture, which used a heavy, wheeled plow whose share had to be supplemented by a mouldboard that turned the furrow completely over. Each kind of plow had a corresponding field shape. Scratch plow cultivation commonly required cross-plowing to assure proper preparation of the soil. Thus squarish field shapes were appropriate for its operation. The mouldboard plow, in contrast, was difficult to maneuver. Four or even six animals were needed to pull it, and such a team required several yards of "headland" on which to turn around. The only efficient way to use such a device was to keep on plowing straight ahead for as long as the lie of the land and the strength of the animals permitted. This, it turned out, was about an eighth of a mile; i.e., the 220 yards of the standard English acre. Elongated strips as against squarish field shapes, therefore, showed which kind of cultivation prevailed in any particular locality. Bloch organized his book around this distinction, for other aspects of rural life all depended on, or were related to, the mode of tillage.

In general, Bloch emphasized stability more than change. He was interested in "les caractères originaux" after all, and so had much to say about internal colonization in France between the eleventh and fourteenth centuries. He took the division between mouldboard and scratch plow cultivation pretty much for granted, without raising the question of whether the one had supplanted the other at some time in history. But his text gave plenty of clues. He recognized that the scratch plow was the older of the two styles of tillage, and emphasized that the long acres of northern France were only part of a much larger region of Germanic Europe in which the same regimen prevailed. And he suggested that in one small corner of France the long acres had indeed supplanted the scratch plow type of cultivation when the superior results Danish settlers attained by use of the mouldboard became apparent to Norwegian and Swedish settlers who, on first lodgment in Normandy, had laid out square fields for the only kind of plow they knew, the old-fashioned scratch plow.

I fairly pounced on this suggestion. It offered a brand new angle of vision on the question that had arisen in my mind a year earlier while reading Cumont, for if the mouldboard plow had supplanted scratch plows not only in Normandy but elsewhere in Europe, then the contrast between the waterlogged plains of

Roman Belgium and the smiling fields of the high
middle ages might be due to the new plow. The hypothesis came, as such things do, in a flash. When in
1983 I looked again at Bloch's pages to remind myself
of what had seemed so immensely exciting in 1939, I
was surprised to see how casual his remark about Normandy was—a single paragraph, tossed off as a mere
guess, needing to be checked against local place names,
and interesting to him mainly as a possible way of dif-
ferentiating initial Norwegian and Swedish from
Danish settlements! Perhaps, as a French patriot, Bloch
did not want to emphasize Germanic contributions to
French society. At any rate, by limiting his attention to
France, he had no occasion to discourse on the original
invention of the mouldboard plow, nor to declare at
what time it first became important for Europe as a
whole. That had happened beyond French borders in
the flatlands of west Germany soon after the beginning
of the Christian era, as I eventually figured out for
myself.

Full understanding did not come all at once. Some
six months of chasing through the Cornell stacks were
required before I understood clearly how the operation
of a mouldboard plow established an artificial system of
drainage in flatlands by producing an elongated grid of
alternating ridges and baulks. Having walked behind
my grandfather's plow helped, for I could summon to
mind a visual image of how the furrow flowed from a
moving mouldboard, tipped to one side and then rolled
over by the action of the plow. It was therefore possible
to see that as plow teams plodded the length of the
long-acre fields, to and fro, the moving mouldboard,
being affixed to one side of the plow, rolled the furrows

over first in one direction, then in the other, thus piling them inward toward the center of each plowland. Repeated plowing could therefore raise the crown of each plowland as high as the plowman desired; while at the outer edges there remained a shallow ditch whence the last furrow had been scraped. The plow's action thus created an effective drainage system for waterlogged land. Successful cultivation of northwest Europe's low lying plains rested on that simple fact. In so moist a climate, drainage was as important as tillage. And that was what the new kind of plowing provided.

To grasp the wider implications of my discovery, I had to explore the chronological and geographical limits of mouldboard cultivation. Working it out gradually permitted me to understand how the long-acre style of cultivation allowed cereal grasses, whose natural habitat was in the semiarid steppe lands of the Near East, to penetrate a brand new ecological niche in the utterly different environment of northwestern Europe. Walter of Henley, a thirteenth-century English agricultural writer, tells it all in Caput 51:

> And when your groundes are sowen, cause the marryshe landes and the waterie landes to be well forrowed and make the water forrowes good and large so that the grounde may be delyvered from the water.[2]

When I found that passage I rested my case. The question about what had happened to Roman Belgium

2. Dorothea Oschinsky, *Walter of Henley and Other Treatises on Estate Management and Accounting* (New York: Oxford University Press, 1971), p. 323.

to make it and adjacent lands along the English Channel and North Sea coasts into the material support for Gothic cathedrals had been adequately answered. So I wrote it all up in a sixty-page paper titled "The Year A.D. 1000" and submitted it, along with another on "The Springs of Plato's Thought" to a prize competition held at Cornell every spring.

I won no prizes and never showed either essay to my professors, nor to anyone other than the anonymous jury. My interests had diverged from those of my teachers, and I may have feared that they would react negatively to my ideas. On the other hand, if Laistner or Stephenson had really liked what I had to say, presumably I realized that to work either theme out properly would require at least a Ph.D. thesis. But I wanted to become a modern historian and had come to Cornell to work with Becker. Moreover, I lacked sufficient Greek and Latin to thrive as a classicist or medievalist, and was not ready to invest the time and effort needed to master the ancient languages.

Obviously, my effort to follow the history of the mouldboard plow, from the time of its emergence among the west Germans in the first Christian centuries until the boundaries of its practicable use had been attained, acquainted me with European geography rather more intimately than before. From "far above Cayuga's waters," I found myself digging into Europe's medieval mud, excited at the thought of how anonymous pioneers had altered the natural topography of the land. It was a great experience.

Actually, the spread of mouldboard cultivation across the plains of northwestern Europe was as drastic a change of natural landscapes as the spread of paddy fields was in south central China and other regions of the Far East. The Chinese ecological breakthrough had occurred a few centuries earlier than the beginning of the mouldboard technique of cultivation, but it proceeded simultaneously with the European agricultural transformation throughout the first Christian millennium. China's incipient world dominance and technical leadership between 1000 and 1500 and Europe's more familiar world dominion between 1500 and 1914 are certainly related to the offset rhythms of their respective agricultural-ecological breakthroughs. But such a concept of world balances is something I have come to only in recent years.

Nevertheless, by the spring of 1940, with Marc Bloch's help, I had discovered a base for European history of a sort I found profoundly satisfying. It rested on an appreciation of everyday routines as pursued by the overwhelming majority. In the Middle Ages and for centuries thereafter, eighty-five to ninety percent of the European population worked in the fields. Their way of life and the moral-political universe built upon their experience constituted the basis of European civilization. Even in our own urban age, those same rural residues remain powerful, pervasive, and fundamental. This was the central thesis of Marc Bloch's book. He convinced me of it in 1939. I am profoundly grateful to him for it.

So pleasing was this sort of vicarious delving into the earth that when it came time to think about a Ph.D. dissertation, I chose to investigate the spread of potatoes, considering that this was the most important change that had come to European agriculture in modern times. In fact, of course, I began with Ireland and never even got to Britain, much less to mainland Europe. Moreover, by the time my thesis was completed, I had become impatient of the excruciating dullness of the sources I had to use. Endless pamphlets and disquisitions by seventeenth- and eighteenth-century improvers became even duller when supplanted in the nineteenth-century by government statistics and official investigations of Irish poverty. I was therefore disinclined to pursue the subject to its original purpose; i.e., to show how the spread of potatoes undergirded the nineteenth-century industrialization of Europe by expanding local food supply, sometimes as much as four times over the caloric yield obtainable from grain harvests of the same fields. I preferred the Toynbeean-Thucydidean vision of the whole, and so set out to write what turned into *The Rise of the West*.

It was toward the end of that enterprise, about 1957 or 1958, that I finally caught up with Braudel by reading *La Méditerranée et le monde Méditerranéen à l'époque de Philippe II*. It was a delight, both for its deft exposition of the variety of human adaptations to Mediterranean landscapes and for its innumerable sidelights on matters previously unknown to me—things like the Ottoman Empire's vain but valiant effort to counter the Portuguese in the Indian Ocean, or the trans-Saharan trade in salt and gold that contributed so much to North Africa's medieval prosperity. A synoptic vision of the Mediterranean Sea and of lands adjacent thereto, running freely across political and cultural boundaries, was just the sort of broad-gauged history I myself was striving for. Here was a man who had achieved it magnificently, sketching a dazzlingly persuasive, impressively learned, and delightfully literate portrait of Christendom's chief zone of interaction with Islam, which was both more finely nuanced and more all-embracing than anything I had ever encountered before.

Of the many books I consulted in the ten years it took to write *The Rise of the West,* Braudel's masterpiece impressed me most. Consequently, when Cass Canfield of Harper's casually asked me over lunch one day who mattered most among contemporary historians, I replied "Braudel." Perhaps he had not heard the name before; at any rate, I had to spell it out before he was satisfied. Yet that casual conversation—no doubt reinforced by other investigations on Mr. Canfield's part—in due course bore quite considerable fruit. For Harper's published a translation of Braudel's book in 1972, thus in effect introducing him to the English-speaking world some twenty-three years after the work had first appeared.

Parenthetically, let me say that the helter-skelter happenchance whereby translation into English of important books from foreign languages now occurs is an unnecessary weakness of our academic life. In the 1940s, for example, Max Weber became a name to conjure with in our universities once his chief works were translated some twenty years after his death; and Braudel has enjoyed a similar, though perhaps less far-ranging, afterburn in this country since 1972. But to depend on an editor's entrepreneurship and the gossip of a chance encounter to determine when and whether great books get translated seems absurd. Some deliberate effort to identify important works, field by field, ought to make it possible to pick up such landmarks not more than five years after their initial publication. If all such books were then promptly and competently translated, English would at once become a second language for all the world, as it already is in many subjects. All we need is a little organization, and modest subventions for translators. Our "Big Foundations" should have addressed themselves to the task years ago. Establishing a lingua franca for all the earth would surely be an unmitigated good. It would safeguard Anglophones from parochialism—what, for example, are Japanese historians up to today?—and enormously improve learned communication across linguistic barriers. It might even make crosscultural misunderstandings more precise and more amenable to debate. But I digress.

However impressive I found Braudel's great book, and however delightful, it remains true that I came upon it too late for it to alter my ideas in any important way. That is a price one pays for growing up, and for having, in the process, made definite commitments as to how best to understand the world. In 1957 I was forty years old, already formed. Of course, a few individuals do undergo conversion experiences after that age, as happened to Toynbee, for instance. But suffice it to say that Braudel did not convert me. What happened instead was that his book brought vividly to my attention a problematic range of phenomena that my earlier habits of thought had disregarded. Dazzlement and puzzlement resulted; and I remain dazzled and puzzled still. This simply means that I am unwilling and perhaps also unable to abandon my own scheme of understanding, but have come to recognize that it leaves out what Braudel has accustomed us to call *conjonctures;* that is, these medium-term fluctuations of economic, demographic, and other circumstances that powerfully affect human life, although they quite escaped contemporary consciousness and can only be detected by painstaking study of statistical data series and other indirect evidences.

My youthful encounter with Marc Bloch had prepared me for Braudel's *longue durée.* The first part of *La Méditerranée,* in which Braudel explores human geography so skillfully, was therefore a pure delight to read, bringing new depth to my conceptions of the dynamics of Mediterranean life—as much in the twentieth century as in the sixteenth. Braudel improved on Bloch's analysis of Mediterranean reality not only through the richness of his details and scope of his description, but also by leaving French national borders far behind and treating the Mediterranean lands as a whole. Moreover, after reading Braudel's account of Mediterranean society I was able to put things I myself had seen in rural Greece during and after the war into a far richer context. The seasonal rhythm of symbiosis between shepherds and grain growers, the affinity of herdsmen to traders and to city folk generally, and the way in which breakdown in peaceful exchange relationships between hill and plain provoked organized violence, not just in wartime Greece but generally throughout Mediterranean lands, all became clear as never before.

That first part of *La Méditerranée* is, indeed, marvelous. Its use of apt, telling detail to create a clear vision of vast panoramas far surpasses anything Braudel's predecessors had achieved. On the other hand, the second and third parts of the book are less dazzling. I must confess that when I used *La Méditerranée* in 1957, I entirely failed to recognize the three-tiered pattern of *longue durée, conjoncture,* and *événement* around which Braudel structured his masterpiece. The reason was that I went to Braudel for *my* purposes, not to explore *his* particular way of understanding things. Where I overlapped his sensibilities, nothing but admiration; where he departed from my predilections, not so much dismay as disregard. Such selective receptivity is normal and natural, and I do not really mean to apologize, just to confess to it.

More interesting is to ask what it was that blunted the impact of Braudel's conjunctures on my thinking; for it is here, not at the level of events, that Braudel had things to teach which I was not ready to learn. Reflecting on this question, it seems to me now, twenty-five years afterwards, that my view of history, ever since encountering Bloch, had focused mainly on changes in the *longue durée.* I was interested in those critical seismic changes that come to human life when something new enters massively into the arena of thought and action, altering older ways of doing things, of thinking, and of interacting with one another. Braudel's book also focused on one such change: the eclipse of Mediterranean primacy by northwestern Europe that took place at the very end of the sixteenth and beginning of the seventeenth centuries. But my effort to understand such changes remained almost wholly at the level of conscious behavior, whereas

Braudel's explanations emphasized trends and circumstances of which contemporaries were completely unaware. I had been perfectly content to share such unawareness because anthropologists had convinced me that changeability in human communities could best be attributed to exposure to strangers bringing unfamiliar skills and ideas to the (often reluctant) attention of those they meet. This was the simple organizing principle behind *The Rise of the West,* and it served me well in bringing intelligible order to the otherwise unmanageable complexity of world history.

What, then, about Braudel's conjunctures? Those patterns of ebb and flow, usually economic, that were not the result of anyone's conscious decision, but which nevertheless could and did profoundly affect the results of conscious undertakings, either forwarding or hindering them systematically? What about other, nonhuman circumstances? Weather, for instance; or epidemiology? And above all, what about business cycles and the rather mysterious Kondratieff waves lasting half a century or so? What, indeed?

Braudel's conjunctures range from economics to what he labels politics, civilizations, and wars; but I think it fair to say that all are based on and related to economic fluctuations. I, on the contrary, have tended to resist the habit of explaining all that happens in economic terms, believing in rather greater autonomy of religious, political, familial, and other forms of noneconomic behavior. Of course there can be no absolute autonomy. Pursuit of noneconomic goals will always have an economic aspect; no one lives for long without food and other material supports of life. But given minimal access to the necessary input of matter and energy, human beings are capable of pursuing quite divergent lines of activity, and do so according to custom and conscious choice. The resulting cultural diversity shapes the economic order within which populations live quite as profoundly as economic constraints shape their deliberate, conscious activities. Or so I am prepared to argue.

Braudel's persistent economic bias registers the degree to which he was impressed by the sovereignty of the market in ordering human affairs, always and everywhere. Perhaps he is a prisoner of the age he chose to concentrate on; that is, early modern Europe, when world-girdling capitalism and an unusually uninhibited pursuit of pecuniary gain *did* prevail, more than usual, over alternative ways of ordering life and channeling human activity. But that remains only a phase of world history, not its universal condition. Moreover, even during that age of triumphant capitalism, alternative ideals—religious, political and professional— all competed with and often deflected market behavior from paths defined by maximal pecuniary gain.

This, however, becomes an argument with contemporary economists as much as with Braudel. My point is rather this: when I first read *La Méditerranée* I confronted a way of understanding history for which I was unprepared. The notion that there are patterns to which human behavior conforms despite contemporary ignorance of them was entirely congenial. But the only such pattern that had attracted my attention in writing *The Rise of the West* was political; the same political motif which Toynbee had used to organize his understanding of human history. For Toynbee's universal states arose when, after a period of intensifying warfare among a number of rival polities, a marginal "marcher" state succeeded in conquering all the rest. The rise first of Macedon and then of Rome, completing the pattern of politics Thucydides had so poignantly analyzed in his book, is the classical case. Close parallels can be found in the history of ancient China and India, among the Amerindians of Mexico and Peru, and in the political evolution of modern Europe. For the eclipse of Italian city-state sovereignty after 1494 and the eclipse of European national sovereignty in our own time through entanglement with polyethnic demicontinental states on either flank—the USA and the USSR— exemplify the marcher state syndrome unambiguously.

Of all this I was well aware, and I had also begun to recognize changing patterns of exposure to diseases which I later explored and wrote about in *Plagues and Peoples*. But there was no place in my scheme of things for Braudel's economic conjunctures. As a result, I disregarded them. That is the fashion in which mature scholars normally treat one another, and explains why book reviews so seldom do justice to really important works that break away from established patterns of thought.

The limits of intellectual discourse between persons whose minds have already been made up was further illustrated by what transpired—and failed to transpire—when Braudel and I finally met face-to-face. This occurred in 1968 when he came to Chicago for a quarter to conduct a "colloque" and to receive an honorary degree. He had just published the first volume of his second magnum opus, *Civilisation matérielle et capitalisme: XV–XVII siècle,* and was working away on its continuation, which finally came out eleven years later in 1979. Braudel's *Material Civilization* is a world history, or purports to be. My own book had come out five years before. One might, therefore, have anticipated a real meeting of minds, or at least serious discussion of how we had respectively sought to reduce the infinite complexity of global experience to intelligible form. Nothing of the sort took place. We did engage in a ritual exchange of books, he giving me a copy of his new *Civilisation matérielle* "en témoinage de réconnaissance et d'affection" and I reciprocating with a copy of *The Rise of the West.* He must have read a few pages of my book. A few days afterwards he even invited me to write a volume on ancient times for a series he was editing. I declined, for the beginnings of civilization was not my thing, and, as Braudel made engagingly clear, this was a choice of desperation on his part, since he had not been able to find a real expert who would take on the task. Still, it was nice to be asked, and I presume that what provoked him to make the offer was a more or less favorable judgment of what he saw in my first few pages.

As for Braudel's gift to me, I regret to say that it struck me as sadly inferior to *La Méditerranée.* The pointillist technique that he had used to such exquisite effect in portraying the Mediterranean world he knew so well lost its magic when applied to the less familiar scenes of East Asia, India, Africa, and America. His choice of tidbits to record seemed whimsical and jumbled. No credible whole emerged. All too often,

indifference to the nonmaterial level of life—the cultural choices and conventions that non-European peoples had inherited from their distant pasts—blunted the delicacy of Braudel's touch. His self-imposed limitation to material life cut off too many human realities; and a profoundly European bias pervaded his work. As my disappointment in his new book became clear, I put it aside and, truth to tell, read it through for the first time in preparation for this lecture.

His treatment of my book presumably conformed to a similar rhythm, for he, too, was uninterested in new architectonic ideas, being far too busy with research on his projected second volume. Coming to Chicago made next to no difference in his pattern of work. That had been defined in his twenties, when, as a lycée teacher in Algeria, he found himself remote from libraries and archives while stubbornly clinging to the aspiration of becoming a university professor. The solution was to devote the necessarily abbreviated time he could spend in archives to photographing vast quantities of documents. He used a primitive motion picture camera acquired from a wandering American at a bargain basement price. He and his wife were then able to spend their spare time all year round accumulating the raw material for the great work he had begun to project.

*Civilisation matérielle,* addressing an even larger canvas than before, demanded even greater diligence. But given a stock of microfilms and a pair of portable microfilm readers, Braudel and his wife were prepared to carry their researches anywhere that electric current was to be had. Accordingly, coming to the American midwest involved no interruption of familiar routine. His bags fairly bulged with films, and his wife was able to set up their portable readers on the day they arrived. Obviously, with such a regimen, there was no time for thinking new thoughts. By then, Braudel had reached the ripe age of 66 and knew that the successful completion of his second great undertaking would require all his energies and those of his wife for years ahead. It is nice to know that he achieved his goal by publishing not one but two fat concluding volumes in his seventy-eighth year, titled respectively *Les Jeux de l'échange* and *Le Temps du monde*.

In some measure, Braudel's visit to Chicago was part of a campaign, nurtured more by his wife than by Braudel himself, to extend his intellectual following to the Anglophone world. He had risen to the top of the academic ladder in France soon after the publication of *La Méditerranée* in 1949, and as editor of the *Annales* had made it the most influential historical journal in the world. By the 1960s he had numerous followers and admirers in Spain, Italy, Latin America, and Poland. Germany and England lagged behind in responding to Braudel's vision of history and historical learning, but the United States was more promising. A few American students had come to Paris to sit at his feet, and did what they could to propagate his approach on returning to this country. Still, as long as his books remained available only in French, most American historians were unable or unwilling to engage seriously with Braudel's way of doing history. Negotiations for translation of *The Mediterranean* were, however, in process, or perhaps they only began during his stay in the

United States—I do not know the facts. At any rate, his benign presence and missionary impulse were much in evidence during his visit to Chicago. He was on the qui vive for students who might come to Paris to work under his aegis; and offered rolls of microfilm from his stock in hand to start them on their way—all with a generosity of spirit and affability of manner that must have done much to sustain his remarkable ascendancy throughout the Francophone world. Unfortunately, his stay at Chicago was cut short by student uprisings in France, and Braudel was suddenly summoned home. His hasty departure nipped his efforts at student re-cruitment in the bud. From that point of view he must have counted his visit a failure.

His colloque was an interesting cross-cultural venture. Braudel, though fully able to make himself understood, refused to speak in English, probably because he did not wish to surrender the ease and elegance that distinguished his spoken as well as his written French. As a result, he cut himself off from all but a handful of our students. On coming into the room, he seemed to start with whatever happened to be uppermost in his mind at the moment, often some detail derived from one of the microfilms he was reading. But his remarks ranged around the world, asking questions more often than answering them, and jesting with us at our inability to respond to problems he raised. For anyone who could follow his words easily, it was a virtuoso performance; but alas, those of our students who could read French often had difficulty following the spoken word, and none of them was exposed long enough to take fire. As for my colleagues, they, like me, were too set in their ways to learn much from Braudel. He therefore left a disappointingly slender trace behind him. The linguistic barrier still held.

Twice subsequently I have met Braudel, but only for short periods of time. The first of these was at a conference in Venice, where I seized the occasion to invite him to write an essay on his view of history and its antecedents for publication in the *Journal of Modern History,* which I then edited. The idea was to launch Braudel's *Méditerranée,* now firmly scheduled for publication in English, with the fanfare it deserved. I proposed to commission two or three review essays on his work to match his own personal testimony, and in fact was able to persuade Hugh Trevor-Roper and Jack Hexter to take on this task. They both rose to the occasion brilliantly.

Braudel hesitated at first, but in due course came through with a splendid self-appraisal, worthy of the historian he is. By good luck all came ready at the end of 1972 just as Harper's published the English translation. So Braudel's masterpiece was properly launched in this country, however belatedly. The train of accidents I have referred to played a larger part than anyone who likes to discern enduring patterns and hidden conjunctures in human affairs is likely to be comfortable with. But no doubt, that is the way things really happen, in small matters as well as in great. Innumerable idiosyncratic personal interactions, after all, underlie and actually constitute what we call history. Words and abstractions merely give form to the inchoate multiplicity of interpersonal transactions, of which this

partial record of my encounters with Braudel is a tiny sample.

Not long afterwards Braudel's personal interactions with Immanuel Wallerstein and others, perhaps just as accidental in origin, led to the establishment of the Fernand Braudel center at SUNY Binghamton. Since then, Braudel's personal reputation and influence in this country have been reinforced and in some degree perhaps also diluted by translations of the work of some of his distinguished colleagues and successors—Emmanuel Le Roy Ladurie first and foremost among them. Yet it seems clear that effective interaction between American historians and the French *Annalistes* has yet to occur, save on a rather superficial level.

A few Americans have attempted to mimic Braudel by borrowing his concepts in toto. This will never work, for it bypasses too much of our own heritage. Moreover, such imitators, almost by definition, are not historians of the first rank, else they would not be content with slavish imitation, even of a master. What we need instead is constructive *mis*understanding of what Braudel has to teach us. That is the true attestation of intellectual influence. In particular, a Braudellian sense of place and of the subtleties of ecological-geographical adjustment of society to its physical environment is much to be desired. Likewise, Braudel's conjunctures deserve to be fitted into our habits of mind. But it would be no gain if these sensibilities were purchased at the expense of attention to the conscious levels of human experience and behavior; and Braudel's tendency to reduce everything to economic and market relationships—a tendency far more pronounced in his *Civilisation matérielle* than in the *Méditerranée*—surely ought to be resisted. Fortunately, we have a rich heritage with which to counteract that kind of reductionism. Notions of culture, culture patterns, culture change, and diffusion of culture traits have been stock-in-trade for Anglo-American social scientists for a generation or longer. Putting that idea-world together with the material relationships and exchanges so dear to Braudel's heart is an effort worth making—very much worth making.

Another way to put the problem is to say that we need to explore feedback patterns that tie together the three levels of human affairs that Braudel merely juxtaposed in *La Méditerranée,* and which he deliberately truncated by omitting political events entirely from his second great work. Interaction does occur. No one doubts that. Deliberate actions and conscious decisions sometimes intervene in the enduring and long-range processes of history—with catastrophic force. The trigger, and the mind that guides the finger that pulls the trigger, are quite as important in deciding what happens as is the gun itself or the sources of supply and methods of manufacture of gunpowder and bullet. So an approach to history that systematically denigrates conscious behavior is as deficient in its way as were the dry-as-dust narratives of conscious policy-making against which Braudel and his mentors rebelled so successfully half a century ago.

How to connect the different levels of human existence remains an unsolved problem. We are symbol-using animals, who dwell simultaneously in the noosphere and in the ecosphere. The music of these spheres registers no simple one-way traffic from lower to higher or vice versa. Access to food and other material necessities certainly does set limits to human life; yet new skills perennially alter access routes to earth's material resources and have repeatedly enlarged the stocks of matter and energy available to human beings. Consequently, we have long since transgressed the limits of the ecological niche reserved for animals at the top of the food chain. Our pullulating numbers have sustained, and are sustained by, depredations on other forms of life that entirely exceed the bounds of biological evolution. Cultural evolution—the accumulation of skills and knowledge—is what allowed us to acquire this unique status; and historians who fail to look for the key transitions in the acquisition of such skills are surely missing a major drama—perhaps *the* major drama—of our past.

Yet if this kind of history simply disregards all small-grained narrative of interpersonal transactions, the genesis of new skills and ideas disappears. Both must somehow be kept in view. What we need to think about, perhaps, is the network of communications that surrounds each one of us from birth to death. Messages in and messages out constitute the sum and substance of what anthropologists call culture; and if one wishes to follow the major contours of humanity's adventure on earth, the best organizing principle might be to look for changes in the communications nets within which human lives are led. If we tried to picture what sorts of messages bound individuals to their fellows in past ages, we might be on the track of a more adequate portrait of the past than anything Braudel's simple jux-taposition of *longue durée, conjoncture,* and *événement* achieved.

Here is a challenge for the rising generation of historians to consider. If a few of them also imitate Braudel, Toynbee, and Becker in their efforts to expand the horizons of the meaningful past to embrace humanity entire, then the study of history will indeed be in good hands. Historians will thereby show themselves willing to meet the needs of our age—needs that arise both from the internal development of our historiographical tradition and from the course of public affairs. I commend the task to those of you young enough to take new ideas seriously and to think anew about the really important questions of human life. It is a great and holy calling. Each of the historians I have here discussed took their calling seriously. So do I. I am confident that our heirs and successors will do the same.